For the Love of Restaurants

An Insider's Guide from Daydreams to Opening Night

Adam Weisblatt

MATT HOLT

Matt Holt Books
An Imprint of BenBella Books, Inc.
Dallas, TX

The events, locations, and conversations in this book while true, are re-created from the author's memory. However, the essence of the story, and the feelings and emotions evoked, are intended to be accurate representations. In certain instances, names, persons, organizations, and places have been changed to protect an individual's privacy.

Matt Holt is an imprint of BenBella Books, Inc.
BenBella Books, Inc.
8080 N. Central Expressway
Suite 1700
Dallas, TX 75206
benbellabooks.com
Send feedback to feedback@benbellabooks.com

Printed in the United States of America
10 9 8 7 6 5 4 3 2 1

Library of Congress Control Number: 2026005006
ISBN 9781637748947 (hardcover)
ISBN 9781637748954 (electronic)

Editing by Katie Dickman
Copyediting by Scott Calamar
Proofreading by Michael Fedison and Sarah Vostok
Text design and composition by PerfecType, Nashville, TN
Cover design by Davin Sanchez and Morgan Carr
Cover and interior illustrations by Davin Sanchez
Printed by Lake Book Manufacturing

Praise for *For the Love of Restaurants*

"Adam is a genuine example of 'go where you wanna go, do what you wanna do, and kick rocks to all the haters.' For Last Word Hospitality, he's the kite and I'm the string and I wouldn't have it any other way. We've been in business together for more than a decade, and it still feels like we're just getting started. Because we are. *For the Love of Restaurants* will give you an inside look at how we got here, where we're going, and how you can blaze your own trail."

—Holly Fox, Cofounder, Last Word Hospitality

"I don't necessarily love restaurants. I love people, and restaurants are full of them. Adam has always seen the beauty in restaurants as living organisms, from the surly bartender to the guest sitting next to him. He belongs. We all do. Reading this book is like sitting and talking with him at the corner of the bar. And Adam can talk. And we've sat there talking about restaurants for hours, because that's what we love."

—Joe Laraja, Cofounder, Found Oyster
and Queen's Raw Bar & Grill

"Nobody loves restaurants the way Adam does. He doesn't just believe in them; he believes in what they mean—to a neighborhood, a culture, the people who walk through the door, and the team who makes it happen every day. *For the Love of Restaurants* captures what most people never see: the risk, responsibility, and conviction behind every meaningful place. If you care about food, small business, or the future of your neighborhood, this book will fundamentally change the way you think about going out to eat and drink."

—Melissa Lopez and Mike Santos, Chef,
Operator, and Partners, Barra Santos

"One thing I'm sure of is that Adam and Holly had their first Last Word cocktail in the dark vestiges of my first bar, The Varnish in Downtown Los Angeles. And albeit he keeps me around because he still can't make one on his own, there is no one like Adam who can speak with facility, specificity, and unapologetic grace on the topic of running a restaurant and how it impacts the community on both sides of the bar. Give this read a rip and learn why who you support when you go out to eat and drink has a major impact on the world at large. Wanna change things? Start local."

—Eric Alperin, Author, *Unvarnished*, and Cofounder, Day By Day Hospitality, the Red Dog Saloon Pioneertown, and The Copper Room

"Adam is, without question, the most passionate person about restaurants that I've ever met—it's almost as if he sees the world through restaurant-colored lenses. He's been an incredible partner and watching him effortlessly practice his craft is a constant inspiration. But what truly sets him apart is his deep care for the industry itself. He believes restaurants are more than businesses; they're community anchors and a way to understand culture, place, and people. Whether you're getting into the business or are simply curious about the inner workings, this book will certainly change your perspective on restaurants, how to run them, and what they mean for the cities and communities they serve."

—Matt and Mike French, Cofounders, Life and Times, the Pioneertown Hotel, and Captain Whidbey

"Adam is a man of strong beliefs. He has a plethora of knowledge from a lifetime of experiences, highs and lows, and a true believer in what restaurants are capable of. He serves no BS and his understanding of hospitality and how to execute it as a genuine human being is bar none, leading to the cultlike following of his restaurants that seem to always be bangers. Adam's know-how on this topic will be eye opening to many and I for one can't wait to see more people understand what goes into the building of an everlasting restaurant."

—DK Kolender and Chelsea Pitts, Chef, Operator, and Partners, Hermon's

"There are few people whose instincts I trust more than Adam when it comes to restaurant operations because I know he has seen it all. If you even think you remotely want to open a restaurant one day, listen to what Adam has to say and maybe you'll save yourself some money in the process and learn something important about why we do what we do."

—Johnny Lee, Chef and Owner, Rasarumah

"Being friends with Adam for more than two and a half decades comes with inside knowledge: The road to restaurateur was inevitable. The late nights in college binge watching Bourdain, Attell's *Insomniac*, *Top Chef*, or the deep discussions on recent meals was just research into how to create the best and most welcoming experience for all diners. Throw in Adam's drive and commitment and the success of Last Word Hospitality should come as no surprise. The fact he's articulated his path for future success stories only solidifies his passion for the industry—do yourself a favor and give this book a read."

—Justin Barry, Friend, Avid Eater, and Private Investor

"I want to stand on the mountaintops and shout with cupped hands that Adam Weisblatt knows everything . . . The company that Holly and Adam have built together is built on people and treating those people with the utmost respect. If you've ever been in the trenches with Adam in life or work, you know he is someone you will always want by your side and on your team. The world according to Weez (his nickname in our Masshole clan) can be bought in hard copy or electronic downloads from anywhere and everywhere your boots, flip-flops, and bare feet touch the terra firma of thy Planet."

—Chris DiGuiseppe, Scholar, Mere Mortal, and Friend

"*For the Love of Restaurants* isn't a glossy restaurant memoir or a dry business textbook; it's a new kind of playbook—a cookbook built from real stories, hard mistakes, loyalty to employees, and foundational principles that apply far beyond the kitchen. I work with entrepreneurs every day in my professional life as a wealth manager, and the constants shared by those that succeed are that they possess the grit to focus on process and persistence. I am proud to have known him for over two decades, have him as a groomsmen in my wedding, and run strategy and ideas by him on a regular basis (albeit two different worlds)—because he is grounded by principle, community, and a desire to learn, understand, and explore all while baking into thoughtful advice to better those around him.

—Dan LaBroad, Managing Director and Private
Client Advisory, Gateway Financial Partners

For the Love of Restaurants

For Owen Arlo and Leah June

And for Mike Simari

And for Jeffery Murphy

CONTENTS

If you want to learn the science of martial arts, meditate on this book; let the teacher be the needle, let the student be the thread, and practice unremittingly.

—Miyamoto Musashi,
The Book of Five Rings, 1643

CV

My first job was waiting tables at the Ground Round—a regional chain that served ice cream sundaes in mini baseball helmets and where kids paid their weight on Sundays. And yes, *we weighed kids.* It was the early 2000s, suburban Massachusetts. At first, I carried a cocktail tray with two hands and used it like a bumper car to clear table space. Delivering drinks I'd never heard of and smiling like a donkey, blindly ignorant of my technically deficient service skills. I've been in the business ever since, mostly the front of house, practicing and making a living and getting better all the time.

I learned that a coffee stirrer will expand the surface area of a liquid. Laid flat, crossing the rim of an overflowing martini, the extra meniscus allows one to navigate even the most chaotic of dining rooms. Even with children skittering like sand crabs around one's feet. And mostly served to patrons who are blissfully unaware of the miraculous powers of physics the simple act of delivering cocktails often requires.

I learned that when triple sat, one should approach the *most recent* table to sit *first.* Make small talk and push for a drink order. Then hit the middle table. Again, a little chitchat and another push for beverages. Then, approach the *first* table to sit. They may be aggravated but charm their little pants off and push for a drink *and* food order. Appetizers will do just fine. Go to the POS terminal and enter the *first* table to sit *first*. Then the second. Then the third. Drinks and food will come out sequentially with how the tables were seated. Then move on to whatever comes next. For there is always something coming next in restaurants.

I learned what it's like to disintegrate the cork of a morbidly expensive bottle of wine in front of its mortified owners. To be eviscerated by a chef, in front of my peers, for mispronouncing "all'Amatriciana" to a group of wholly unconcerned guests.

I learned what it's like to subsist on clam chowder mixed with lobster bisque, sipped from little paper ramekins, while working back-to-back-to-back "clopener" doubles.

And I learned the sensation of being jolted awake, drenched in sweat and overwhelmed with burning futility, exclaiming in defeat, "I forgot the *fucking mustard* for that woman on table seventeen!," only to have a similar epiphany the following night. And the night after that.

I've served celebrities. Famous chefs. Food critics. Tables of drunk bachelorettes. Tables of drunker bachelors. Tables of biker gangs.

I've been stiffed. Insulted. Tormented. Belittled. Built up. Knocked down. Charmed. Brought home. Told that I was special. Told that I absolutely sucked. I've waited tables. Managed bars. Consulted on restaurant operations. And played one role or another in dozens of restaurant openings—a subgenre of restaurant work I became uniquely fond of.

You see, opening a *new* restaurant is an experience like no other. And the creation of these multidimensional worlds—*real worlds*—is the work I became most fascinated with doing. It's one thing to work in an established restaurant, already in its groove and operationally molded to serve its patrons. It's quite another to look upon an empty room of concrete, drywall, and decrepit plumbing and envision how a complicated performance of cooking, serving, dining, and cleaning could take place there. *Imagining* what future guests would be attracted to. What they would *love.* And what they would return to. To hatch a living, breathing place from an empty shell of a building. A place to be shared. A place filled with human beings, *simply enjoying life*. It's a journey I never tire of.

And twenty-five years after starting out, I now co-own and operate seven unique restaurants in Southern California. One could even forgive me for saying that they are seven *celebrated* restaurants. And I'm not alone in this endeavor, thank god, but rather, I am in the far more enviable position of having a group of partners whom I genuinely love spending time with. But how will our collective ventures fare in the future? Well, I'd be a damn liar if I told you I knew with any certainty. The restaurant business is tough. And it will always be tough.

In this book, I'll share with you all that I know about what it takes to imagine, conceptualize, design, build, launch, and operate a restaurant. But rather than bounce from story to story, and restaurant to restaurant, I've focused the narrative and curriculum on a single opening. A single opening in which every aspect of our process for making new *places* will be revealed.

And although I can share no secret ingredient to opening a restaurant successfully—for in this business, *everything* matters—if I were to share anything useful in this brief introduction, it would be that resilience, creativity, empathy, and, maybe most importantly, the people around me are what steered my fate.

This is a book about restaurants. And a book about people. And, maybe, a book about life.

I hope you enjoy reading,
Adam

•1•

Finding Love in an Empty Room

Site Inspection #373.

Or so it felt . . .

"Holy shit . . ." Holly whispered. "Adam, look where we are."

"*Whoooaaa* . . ." I craned my neck upward as we walked. "Well, at least *everybody* knows where this is . . ."

Holly held her gaze. "Yeah . . . I suppose that's true . . ."

The building at 4880 Fountain Ave lived in the hulking shadow of the big blue mother ship of Scientology.

Originally an Art Deco hospital complex, the religious vessel occupied an entire city block. Emblazoned S-C-I-E-N-T-O-L-O-G-Y, each letter the size of an Escalade, the imposing structure left no passerby in doubt of its proprietor. From its iron-gated gut, a cement staircase descended onto Fountain Ave like the unfurling gangway of a UFO. And hustling intently, as if Big Blue would depart the mortal world at any moment, the guardians of Scientology circled the block on entirely Earth-based, non-ethereal, black bicycles.

"I do like the security guards," I muttered under my breath.

"You *like* the security guards?" Holly replied, searching for my second head.

"A server walking to their car late at night—"

"*Gotcha* . . . You're always imagining the worst . . ."

"It's true, Holly Fox. The worst, I can always imagine."

For more than a year, Holly and I had been seeking a location to build our first restaurant—a neighborhood oyster bar.

But convincing ourselves to say yes to a space had proven a difficult argument to win. At first, we'd concentrated on sites with past restaurant lives. But those spaces required cash up front, a fee paid to an existing tenant or landlord known as "key money." And cash up front, well, that was simply not an option. The space at 4880 Fountain Ave had never been a restaurant before, making it more likely to be acquirable, and rentable, within our admittedly limited budget. We'd been told it had great bones. And that it was small. We were looking for small.

We passed a row of olive trees as we completed our exodus through the land of Scientology, crossed two narrow lanes of Fountain Ave, and approached a timeworn, gray brick building. A decaying security enclosure and a tattered yellow "Space Available" banner hid an Edward Hopper storefront of antiqued wood and glass. To the left of the single-story structure was an aging bodega. To the right, an empty storefront. I retrieved the key from a lockbox as I'd been instructed by the landlord and wrestled with the now-shrieking steel gate. Holly and I stepped over the rickety threshold, past an apparently burglarized door, under a crumbling air-conditioning unit, and into our future.

"Well . . . It's a long way from being a restaurant . . ." Holly murmured. Her sandy-blonde hair in a ponytail, she wore her typical attire of boyish blue jeans, a white T-shirt, and leopard-print shoes, all with the authority of a royal. A royal with a tape measure.

It took me only a few strides to reach the far end of the shipping-container-shaped room. Looking back toward Holly,

I took in the scenery. Dust-covered linoleum floors, stained Sheetrock walls, office-building ceiling panels, and a swamp of frayed black wiring peeked out from every imaginable orifice. A single, phone-booth-sized bathroom was nestled in the rear corner. I held out my arms like a flying ding-dong, trying to get a scale of the room. "How big do you think it is in here?"

"Oh, gosh. Not more than seven or eight hundred square feet," Holly answered.

"Yeah, that's what I was thinking. *Very* small. But I think she's cute. You think she's cute?"

"It needs a lot of love, Adam. A *lot* of love. But . . . she is cute. Very cute."

I pulled open what remained of the bathroom door with the toe of my boot, caught a whiff of sulfur, and booted it closed with my heel. "Definitely needs a lot of love . . ." I whispered.

Now, as important as any oyster to ever be shucked by a shucker is the room in which that oyster is shucked. And with that weight upon us, Holly and I stood and stared at the dusty shoebox that was 4880 Fountain Ave. Despite the trepidation we felt, a small space was our best chance at opening our own restaurant. And if by some restaurant miracle we managed to pull the whole thing off, a smaller restaurant would need fewer guests to *feel* full. That may sound trivial, but consider that a half-empty restaurant breeds the dangerous feeling of a diner's insecurity; a *full* restaurant, on the other hand, confirms that a diner has made an admirable, crowd-approved choice. Restaurants may sell food and drink, but sustaining the energy of a crowd is the best way to keep the crowd.

Holly finally broke the long silence. "How bad is the bathroom? I need to pee."

"I don't know, Holly. I'd suggest you hold it."

"Gross." Holly giggled. "OK. I think it's darling in here," she said as she took a deep breath and wrinkled her nose. "Not smelling so great at the moment, but it's got great energy. What do you think? You wanna call the landlord?"

"Yeah, I'll call the guy. And who knows? Maybe we'll even find somebody reasonable in charge."

Holly and I had a vision for an oyster bar, but it needed a home. And our restaurant would be no hermit crab. When we chose a space, that would be it. Good or bad, we would be forever tied to that location. I called the landlord the moment we left. Our conversation was brief but amicable. And he came right out with his asking price and length of term. Never one to negotiate over the phone, I requested a meeting. And I requested additional access to the space. Holly and I would now dive into our vetting process. It was time to ponder the universe—and a new oyster bar within it. Moses, the landlord, agreed.

Assessing Terms on *Your Terms*

In your hunt for a restaurant space, know that commercial real estate is typically priced *by the square foot.* And although this approach is inarguably rational from a real estate perspective, determining the viability of *your restaurant* by this same calculation may lead to catastrophe. Restaurants don't make money per square foot. Nor do they make money per seat. Restaurants make money per seat *with asses in them*. You'll be losing money on seats without asses. Remember, bigger spaces are harder to fill, harder to staff, and more expensive to build. Price per foot be damned—the *total* rent owed each month is the only number you need to worry about. And it's the only number that's going to matter at the end of a slow month. So, take your time. Look

> at a lot of spaces. Review a lot of deals. Get a feel for what feels fair. A good deal is the one that works for *you*.

Know Thy Space. Most Intimately . . .

It was with cautious enthusiasm that we set out to understand what it would take to turn 4880 Fountain Ave into the oyster bar we had been dreaming about. Holly and I faced five major risks: the neighborhood, the space, the concept, the operating model, and the lease. Each contributed to the restaurant's viability in its own way. The concept and model, although often viewed as permanent, could be adjusted and tweaked and improved upon in perpetuity. But the neighborhood, the space, and the lease—these were *forever decisions*. And if we decided to set sail from this location, our survival would depend entirely upon the sturdy construction of our little restaurant ship, for even the smallest leak could sink us.

Speaking of ships, it's often said that nothing costs more than maintaining these floating money pits. But the people who say that have never owned a restaurant. And long before investing time into lease negotiations, Holly and I would comb the space in desperate avoidance of investment incinerators—those unavoidable infrastructure improvements that guests would never see, hear, feel, touch, or taste. They have the potential to burn untold stacks of cash with no possibility of a tangible return. Our future patrons would comment on the barstools, but the sewer connection not so much.

It's important to note that Holly and I are not general contractors. Nor are we plumbers, electricians, or architects. We're restaurant people. And five years after starting a small restaurant consulting firm, Last Word Hospitality (LWH), it felt like the time had come to open a place of our own. A place to show all we'd learned and love about restaurants. And years of watching clients struggle with the physical limitations of their spaces had taught us where to focus our attention during these early site inspections. Spaces that had already been restaurants may be considered "grandfathered." And like a wily octogenarian claiming "Bingo!" in a game of bridge, these places are allowed to operate by a less strict interpretation of the rules. New projects are not afforded this latitude. Turning 4880 Fountain Ave into a restaurant would mean complying with current code in every color of the rainbow. And with a tool kit of nothing more than a tape measure, Holly and I set out to determine if 4880 Fountain Ave had the capacity to transform into a restaurant without leaving us flat broke in the process.

During our next visit to the space, Holly stood at the entrance and stretched the measuring tape across the threshold. Her brow wrinkled as I approached. "We've got a bit of a problem over here."

"What's the deal?" I asked.

"This old storefront is *old*. And the doorway isn't wide enough to pass ADA. We're half an inch short." Meeting code requirements of the Americans with Disabilities Act was nonnegotiable, and Holly stretched the measuring tape once again. "Yeah. It's definitely short."

"So, what's that mean for us?"

"There's a distinct possibility that we'll need to replace the storefront."

"I don't like that at all."

"Well, I wouldn't get your hopes up."

But, per usual, I did get my hopes up. The facade was as old as the neighborhood itself, unabashedly charming, and aesthetically important. *There is no fucking way we'd have to replace the storefront*, I thought. Or at least, that's what I chose to believe.

After clearing the invisible minefield of project-killing problems, we investigated the trash situation. The importance of trash storage and removal should never be underestimated. It literally and figuratively stinks when getting rid of refuse is a problem. And I have witnessed entire neighborhoods rise up in pitchfork-carrying revolt against an overflowing rubbish situation. There was a dumpster in the alley behind 4880 Fountain Ave. It was secured behind a black gate and large enough for the daily onslaught of shells, bones, skin, and scales that an oyster bar would create en masse. *Check.*

At the end of our inspection, we felt mostly confident with the extent of upgrades necessary to turn 4880 Fountain Ave into the tiniest of oyster bars. A full suite of tradespeople would be needed to establish the electrical, plumbing, and mechanical requirements of the building, from hand sinks to air-conditioning. That is, in addition to building and equipping a kitchen, a bar, and a dining room, and integrating the little details that would make the place feel like a restaurant and not a car rental office.

To understand how our little oyster bar may fit into the greater community, it was time to take a wider view of our surroundings. We needed to see 4880 Fountain Ave from a bird's-eye view. And we needed to take some time to get a feel for things on the street.

Restaurant Reconnaissance

Holly and I decided it would be prudent, downright critical even, to attempt to eat and drink at every restaurant and bar in East Hollywood. In one night. An R&D *bang, bang, bang, bang, bang* of the highest order. Our expedition commenced with heaping plates of falafel and soujouk sandwiches devoured in faux-wood booths under the watchful gaze of a very large, very sweaty cook at Falafel Arax. Then, literally three steps from door to door, we entered a local Thai food favorite, Spicy BBQ, for a scalding mosaic of khao soi and spicy jackfruit salad. And with my appearance now mirroring that of the aforementioned cook, doused in sweat and with no boozy refreshments to ease my suffering, we went in search of respite.

A five-minute rideshare down the road and we arrived at Tabula Rasa Bar. There, we sat under our first soft lighting of the night. And with glasses of ice-cold wine, we gossiped about how an oyster bar would fit in with the neighborhood's older, proven, and more established peers. We talked about the close proximity between bars and restaurants and the countless apartments filled with potential customers and staff. And we talked about what it would feel like to introduce a very new restaurant to a very old neighborhood. After an hour or so, we continued onward to a hip new restaurant with new-car sparkle. Transplanted from Brooklyn, it was, at that time, the talk of the town.

And so, it came as quite a shock that while entering through a gilded-age doorway I was greeted by a bartender familiar to me. From a local dive, of all places. And as Holly and I took our seats, ordered cocktails and an appetizer of steamed mussels, I couldn't help but feel jarred by this Harley-Davidson of a man working within this brand-spanking-new, fancy-pants cocktail bar. And while we worked our way through unnecessarily complicated and not-quite-chilled cocktails, we waited patiently for our food. And waited. And waited. I noticed an 86 list written in Sharpie taped haphazardly to the bar. *Had a pool hall puked on a palace?* Then, the mussels arrived.

"Whatcha think, guys? Fuckin' great, right?" the bartender inquired. "Those mussels are the shit, huh?" I tried to respond, but my mouth was full. And before I could swallow, he was gone. The mussels, unfortunately, were cold. We paid, tipped like our karma depended on it, and went on our merry way. This one, it wouldn't last.

With a steady buzz now driving us forward, we decided to pay homage to one of the neighborhood's most historic institutions, Jumbo's Clown Room. And after a few beers beneath an inverted, bikini-clad, pole-attached, storm-trooper-helmet-wearing Athena, stomping along the ceiling in goldfish-bowl heels, it was time, once again, to eat. With no dining available at Jumbo's, we headed just a few doors down to another much-beloved Thai restaurant, Ruen Pair. Open late enough for the dancers at Jumbo's to go after work, Holly and I crawled our way inside and ordered a plethora of mouth-burning Thai favorites under eye-burning fluorescent lights. Satay, crab fried rice, molten papaya salad, and one last cold beer all combined into warm, fuzzy, faded memories. All in the name of research, of course.

Now, although not intimately familiar, I knew a bit about East Hollywood. Especially from a restaurant perspective. Angelenos had been traveling to the neighborhood, just to eat, for years. And if you looked at a map, you'd notice East Hollywood as the geographic center of the great sprawl that is Los Angeles. I liked the idea of being within this culinary bull's-eye. East Hollywood was the best neighborhood for Thai food in America. And if it weren't for the neighboring city of Glendale, it may also be the best for Armenian food. There were fantastic spots for Mexican food. Filipino. Korean. Persian. Japanese. Salvadoran. And the typical LA-style variety of 24-hour burger joints and doughnut shops.

For all the amazing meals that could be had in East Hollywood, a dozen oysters and a lobster roll were not one of them. The neighborhood did not have a restaurant like the one that existed in our minds. But could we stand out while fitting in? Was it love—or a passing fling? Making a choice meant taking the bad with the good. Our future would be forever tied to this decision.

Three sheets to the wind and standing in front of 4880 Fountain Ave in the middle of the night, gazing through barred windows and beyond the tattered yellow banner, I thought I saw shuckers twirling in the moonlight . . .

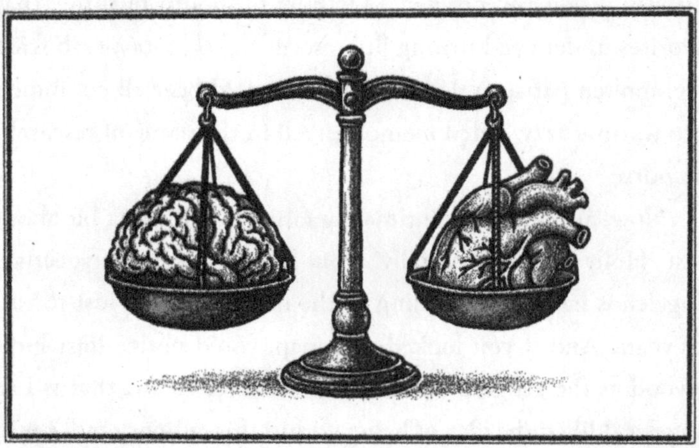

Romance vs. Rationale

Some people may tell you that population density and demographics are deciding factors for a restaurant's location. Others will tell you to go with your gut, assuring you that a tingly kind of feeling will signal when to strike. The answer, for restaurants at least, lies somewhere in the middle. But for all the traffic studies, market analysis, or economic exploration one can go through, there is nothing more important than *fitting in*. My apologies if that sounds like the worst advice to give a middle schooler, but this ain't eighth grade.

This is the restaurant business. And when you open a business with an open door to the street, it's best to feel welcome when you step outside. Data is good. But it should be backed up by spending real time, in the real place, with the real people you will now be neighboring. In a business for which the product is judged by how human beings *feel* when they walk inside, have a meal, and interact with their neighbors, you want to be damn sure that it *feels right*, right from the beginning.

• 2 •

Breaking Down the Big Decision

It was deep within an industrial neighborhood in Downtown LA, through a series of colossal storerooms filled with folded trousers, paper goods, and mountains of lemons and limes, that we first met Moses. Dressed in blue jeans, a mostly unbuttoned button-down, and a gleaming gold necklace with matching watch, he had an ear-to-ear smile that surfaced my heart from my stomach. I liked him immediately.

Moses greeted us warmly as we took our seats around an enormous conference table. We spent some time exchanging pleasantries, his gaze shifting back and forth between Holly and me. Once settled in, we told Moses of our hopes of opening a restaurant at 4880 Fountain Ave.

Moses furrowed his brow and adjusted his watch. "It's *very* small for a restaurant, isn't it?"

"It is," I said, leaning in. "But small is intimate, and LA is a place that lacks intimate spaces. We love that it's small."

"And smaller is cheaper to build, Moses," Holly added.

"Oh, I see. That's very smart, Holly. Very smart. I know restaurants are very risky . . ." Moses made a clicking sound like he was beckoning a horse. "Tk tk tk. And are the two of you married?"

"We're both married, Moses. But not to each other," I replied.

Moses giggled and my fondness for him increased. "*Ha!* OK, I see. So . . . What *kind* of restaurant do you want to build?"

We would now need to convince Moses of the viability of our oyster bar. If a lease was to be signed—"if" being a big "if"—Moses would essentially be our first partner. A vital one. For we knew that Moses's attention would be key in building the restaurant efficiently. And we knew the challenges with 4880 Fountain Ave would not simply cease post launch. Restaurant spaces always have problems. *Always.* Our dealings with Moses would continue into the distant future.

"Well, Moses . . ." I settled into my seat and continued, "We want to do our own version of a New England oyster bar."

"You know, not everybody eats oysters," Moses said, looking cautiously between Holly and me. "A lot of people don't eat oysters. *I* don't eat oysters."

My heart sank back into my gut.

"We know that oysters aren't for everyone, Moses," Holly replied as our eyes met, "but the people that love oysters *love* oysters. And it's just another reason we've been looking for a smaller space. Fewer seats mean fewer butts to be busy."

We spent the next few minutes explaining why we'd chosen an oyster bar over a burger stand or a pizza shop until, finally, we breached the topic at the heart of our entire discussion. *The deal.* Moses repeated the terms he'd quoted over the phone, stressing that it was a "gross lease." A *gross lease* means real estate taxes, property insurance, and common area maintenance are already packaged into the single, monthly payment. A "net lease" would have meant those expenses would be billed *in addition* to the base payment. His was a standard, but fair, offer.

But the *cost* of rent was only half the codfish. I asked Moses what length of term he was willing to offer.

"How would five years work for you?" Moses asked.

"Five years would not work for us, Moses," I answered. Warmly.

Now, as you can probably tell, I don't negotiate like a bully. I employ no powerful hand gestures. I hide no enthusiasm. My poker face is a shit-eating grin. But I'm honest about what I need to make a deal work. And I will walk away from a deal that won't work. Even if I want it. Even if I *really* want it. I asked Moses for a ten-year lease, with two five-year "options." A full two decades at 4880 Fountain Ave. He said he'd have to talk to his partners. And as Holly and I left his office, I asked him to pass along a message: "Moses, when you're talking to your partners, tell them that we'll *always* pay on time. We're going to be in business for years. And we're going to massively increase the value of your building."

Moses smiled wryly at Holly. "What do you think, Holly? Is he right or is he crazy?"

Holly smiled back. "I *know* he's right, Moses. And we'll be the best tenants a guy could ask for."

Everybody was smiling now. Smiling like street fighters.

A few days later, Moses submitted an updated offer. I pushed for better terms but got nowhere. If we wanted to build a restaurant at 4880 Fountain Ave, this was the best we were going to get. And what we were going to get was not quite what we had wanted. The lease would be slightly more expensive, and slightly shorter, than we had hoped. But still, I *liked* Moses. And so did Holly. Moses was an independent operator, a genuine guy, and he was *excited about what we brought to the table*. And we knew that it wouldn't be torture handing over rent every month. That was worth something. Not everything. But something.

Munching the Numbers

At this point, Holly and I had invested only a few hours of work into 4880 Fountain Ave and, aside from a jacked-up credit card from our R&D shenanigans, zero dollars. But if we moved forward, our investment of time and money would increase. So, to aid our decision, we began a series of financial exercises in an attempt to sketch a fiscal picture that was yet to be painted. Holly and I would spend weeks inside a spreadsheet fever dream of estimated financials. And after multiple edits and revisions and re-revisions, we felt confident with our figures. Or at least confident enough to accept the consequences of being wrong.

First, we created a "pre-opening budget." The POB was broken into two main categories, and while most were pornographic in their descriptions, their definitions were far less stimulating. "Hard costs" were the obvious ones: building materials, equipment, labor. Physical, tangible stuff. "Soft costs" were the less obvious ones: legal fees, insurance, city permits. And to further complicate things, we knew that the longer it took us to open, each month of rent would continue to stack against us. *Time* would contribute to the budget as much as physical construction.

Next, we created an "operating budget." The OB, also known as a pro forma, was intended to reveal what it would take to operate the restaurant. And what it would take to earn back what we put into it. If the POB had been a work of tedious research, then the OB was the work of *imagination*. On paper and through numbers, we played pretend restaurant by testing operational theories to *visualize* how sales, expenses, profitability, or potential losses could play out in real life. And the more realistic we were in developing these financial representations, the better prepared we would be to manage that financial picture *if* operations were to truly begin.

Most importantly, we needed to avoid the disaster-developing behavior known as "calculator dreaming." This is a Beach Boys–sounding disease that reveals itself through symptoms easily recognized in statements such as: "They're doing $10 million down the street and that place sucks! I'm *sure* we can do at *least* that much."

You see, a calculator dreamer chooses to use *dreams* as a tool for determining viability. And dreams, if vital for inspiration, are fatal for finances. And if betting on *realistic* projections was good business, betting on these saliva-inducing delusions was a surefire way to end up insolvent. Holly and I *organically* worked through projections. Which is to say, we grew them from seed. How many guests would visit on a Monday? A Friday? What would they spend on dinner? How many cooks would it take to pull that off? Servers? We had to envision ourselves as a deserted island and predict how many folks would paddle ashore.

One tiny piece at a time, we tried to solve the ten-thousand-piece puzzle of building and operating an oyster bar. Pushing covers higher and guest checks lower and then reversing. Assembling hard costs, soft costs, revenue, and expenses into a portrait of financial functionality. And if there was a keystone piece to each iteration we worked through, it was *rent*. Every other number was a fantasy projection and potentially alterable. But *rent* was a number we could predict accurately from day one. If the oyster bar was an experiment, then rent was the control. Everything else would be variable.

When to hold. And when to fold.

Deciding on a restaurant lease is a game of restaurant poker. The pre-opening budget is your stack of chips. The operating budget, your hand. You'll need to weigh the *balance* between the two budgets to decide if it's time to fold or time to play, determining if the cards you're holding justify pushing your stack of chips onto the table. This game is about risk. Risk weighed against reward.

> And the more balanced the bet, the better the bet. What you don't want is to find yourself all in, praying for a royal flush, drinking warm whiskey and sweating bullets and plucking out your eyelashes with all your chips on the table. The trick is betting a stack of chips that is justified by your hand. The hand that you can afford to play. The hand that can be won with no cards to brag about.

Saying Yes Means Embracing the Risk

Risk, like expense, takes many forms—some obvious, some less so. Our reputation would be at stake as much as, if not more than, our money. Five years of building our standing as restaurant consultants washed out with one very visible ass kicking. Launching a restaurant would mean putting our ethos and abilities on public display. And we feared that a failed restaurant would be followed closely by a failed consulting practice. But fear, itself, can be used as fuel.

Restaurants are roller coasters. And like riding a roller coaster, it's important to know you've been strapped into a thrill machine before the big drop. The difference between posing for the descent camera and preparing for a sudden, violent death will determine the condition of your pants at the end of the ride. Meaning, to assume risk blindly and assume risk with forethought are two very different things. One, exhilarating. One, petrifying. So, before climbing aboard, we made one final inspection of the tracks.

Holly and I returned to 4880 Fountain Ave to make our decision. We walked past Big Blue, wrestled the shrieking security gate, passed under the broken air conditioner, and stared at the gray box of a room. If we moved forward, this address would be officially designated as our ol' ball and chain. Now, and forever.

"Well . . ." I sighed.

"Well . . ." replied Holly.

"We've never taken a risk like this."

"I know. Consulting has never been scary. This is scary."

"It is scary. But . . . She is awfully cute."

"Yes. She is very cute."

We continued to stare at the little room. Beneath its unassuming veneer, I could see an oyster bar hiding in plain sight. An open kitchen with oyster-shucking bartenders. They were smiling and pouring wines and working like graceful octopi as they entertained marvelous, laughing, celebrating guests. Lovers rested elbows on the well-worn bar, playing footsie and making their own hazy memories of the restaurant. A room of constant movement. Excitement. Passion. And boundless energy. But it was such a big step to commit to the space.

I slowly became aware that Holly was talking to me. "I think we found it . . . Adam . . . Adam? *I think we found it.*"

I was shocked. Holly had always been the more conservative one. And even though I, myself, had started to believe that *this* might be the right place, I was utterly floored when I heard Holly confirm what I was thinking. I had always assumed I'd need to talk her into signing a lease. But that's not what happened; Holly was ready. We were going to buckle up and ride the coaster. *This was it.*

"Holy shit . . . *Holy shit!* Holly! We found it!"

We both embraced and jumped up and down like two childhood friends who made the varsity softball team together. There may have been a few tears.

After years of looking, we'd finally found our chance.

Our oyster bar had a home. And a name. Holly said it right away and I loved it right away. It was just a feeling. We'd *found* it.

Found Oyster was coming soon.

And I was fucking terrified. I mean, exhilarated! Exhilarated, I say!

Chasing Perfect Is a Road to Nowhere

Before signing a lease for *your* restaurant, you need to understand *exactly* what you're getting and what you're giving up. Are you paying up for a prime location? Or getting a slammin' deal on a riskier address? Does a big patio give you flex space on the weekends? Or does a smaller space create a more intimate experience? Will an injection of cash from the landlord, known as "tenant improvements," or TI, give you the capital to build a killer dining room? Or are you better off avoiding cash from the landlord in exchange for a lower monthly rent? And remember, and I could say this a million times and say it one more time still, regardless of what kind of lease agreement you're signing—for leases can stretch from just a few pages to longer than this book—the *total* amount due each month is what is going to drive the financial reality of your restaurant. And, of course, how well you sleep at night.

So, if you're truly dedicated to bringing something real into this world, something as real as a restaurant, you're going to need to make real sacrifices. And learning how to see the good—and the bad—in every opportunity is the only way to know which opportunity is right. Seek balance. And allow a combination of rational thinking, personal research, and that tingly feeling in your gut to guide your choice. When, after much contemplation and visualization of your future, you do decide upon a road forward, don't be afraid of hitting a few potholes along the way. It's simply part of the journey.

3

Start Up and Survive

Back in the day . . .

I found myself awakening to an obnoxious, repetitious *click*. Assuming it to be the electric heater firing up in my tin-can apartment, I rolled over and tried to pull up my sheets. But much to my surprise, I found that I was seated at a conference table, dressed in a suit, and that I was in the middle of a sentence which I, myself, did not comprehend. A dream, obviously. I rubbed my eyes and attempted once again to roll over and go back to sleep.

But I was still sitting up. And I was still in a suit. And in front of me, my boss, Robert, was glaring into the innermost sanctuary of my soul. His habit of clicking a pen out of pent-up frustration in full effect. Again, I rubbed my eyes. But I could not escape the dream. Robert's stare grew darker, and steam billowed from every pore on his bald head. And as I watched that rice cooker of a noggin, I became aware that the conference table at which I sat was surrounded by my coworkers. Alex the host. Marissa from pastry. Juan the sous chef. Mick the chef. Sally from reservations. Camilla the sommelier. And Robert. Their faces combining into a distorted mix of confusion, humiliation, shock, and desperation. Unable to escape this interstellar nightmare, and unsure if I was witnessing past, present, or future, I decided to play along.

"OK, well. *Um*, well . . . Chef Mick and I have been working on some menu updates. We're really ramping up training and trying to get the staff all buttoned up. I think people are really going to like it. We're uh, we're going to do some trainings . . . We, uh, we . . ."

The pace of Robert's clicking picked up steam. Built like an NFL lineman, he wore an exquisitely manicured, almost waxy goatee that reflected his entire persona. Robert didn't so much scare me as he did throw me into an occasional state of shock. I would become frozen under the hypnosis of his clicking pen.

"Adam, listen to me. And for that matter, *everyone* please listen to me. Come *prepared* to these meetings. Bring your agenda. I expect to hear about the progress *you* are making in the dining room. Or in any department for that matter. And I expect to hear about that progress *every* week. I do *not* want to hear vague rumblings about what you've been up to. You're better than this, Adam." *Clk-clk-clk-clk-clk-clk* . . .

As if it weren't enough to be managing, for the first time, a business that never takes a day off, I had to contend with the severity of my boss. Dragging down the already-leaking dinghy of my self-confidence. And while my job title may have indicated that I was running a restaurant, the truth was more to the contrary. A restaurant was running me and running through my dreams.

The next day, now awake, after the Roman slaughter that was our weekly operations meeting, I broke off to the kitchen with Chef Mick. Dressed in a white, collared dishwasher shirt instead of a chef's coat, Mick was the first chef I'd worked with who hadn't made a habit of torturing the dining room staff. Built like a T-bone steak with eggplants for arms, he was untroubled by Robert's tirade. And as Mick began breaking down a full leg of lamb, carefully slicing off each muscle and placing it lovingly in the macabre arrangement of a meat-based idol, he delivered a sermon that would forever change the way I viewed working in restaurants.

"You gotta remember, Adam. Robert has been doing this for his entire life. Sure, the position of GM sounds nice, but it's a tough gig. Everybody thinks that restaurant jobs get easier as you move up the ladder, but of course, they don't."

"Sure, Mick. But why does he have to be such a dick all the time? It's like he wants to torment us."

"I don't think he wants to torment us, dude. Robert is *overwhelmed*. You don't see it because of the age gap. He's older and you think wiser. But he still hasn't figured this shit out."

Mick was a kinder soul than his kitchen-altered appearance may have indicated. Despite the cuts and burns on his arms and tattoos on his neck, Mick was known for making the entire staff ice cream sundaes after a long shift. For attending his cooks' kids' quinceañeras. And for his off-menu, post-shift, General Tso's chicken. He was very much unlike the previous chef I had worked with, known for his maniacal, tyrannical, hysterical hissy fits and his less-than-loving tendency to emphatically trash perfectly good food rather than feed a front-of-house employee. Mick looked like an MMA fighter. But he had the heart of a kitty.

"Adam, the part of this job that most people never accept is that you simply can't 'win.' There is no 'winning' in restaurants. There are good games and bad games. But there are no championships."

"Winning a Beard would be something, though. Right? Maybe a Michelin star?"

"You think winning an award means something changes? Restaurants get busier, sure. But they *never* get easier. If anything, 'winning' means more expectations. And with those expectations, more stress. Sometimes more money, sometimes not. But *definitely* more stress. Robert was a partner at some great restaurants in NYC, man. But that didn't mean he could sell out and go live on a beach somewhere. This business just isn't like that."

"So, what the fuck are we doing here, Mick?"

"I play restaurants because I like the game. I think Robert lost that love a long time ago. But like a lot of people in this business, he does what he knows. And he never learned that *liking* this job is the only reason to stick with it. For you, buddy . . . well, that's for you to decide."

Returning to my tin-can apartment that evening, I couldn't stop thinking about what Mick had said. Sage-like in his simplicity, Mick had made clear in ten minutes what had been cloudy for ten years: *There is no "winning" in restaurants.* And if there was no winning, then the best anyone could ever do was *play*. I had always loved working in restaurants. Sure, that love was complicated, but when isn't love complicated? Like all relationships, working through the hard times would be more important than finding a flawless match. For such a thing simply does not exist. There would be no "mission accomplished" in my future. No tech titan fortune at the end of the rainbow. If I was going to make my career in restaurants, I needed to make damn sure that I was doing it for *love.*

The "Best" Is a Matter of Personal Taste

The success of a restaurant is determined by its *community.* Not accolades. And while some believe that stars on the wall are the sign of a great restaurant, the rule following required to win these decorations often results in a homogeneous hot mess. The *best* restaurants are the ones that feel the most genuine. They feel like a little piece of the neighborhood. A little piece of their creators. And a little piece of a larger culinary story. So, if you're dedicating huge chunks of your life to restaurants, make sure you're doing it with *passion*. Do it for *your* community. And do it for yourself. People will know if you're sharing something from the heart. They'll recognize it without even knowing how. And in restaurants, with mostly your neighbors walking through that door, they'll know immediately, and with great certainty, who it is you're trying to impress.

Finding a Place to Start. And a Person to Start With.

By 2014, now thirty years old, I had spent half my life working in restaurants. I had slung frozen food from tourist traps. Worn my twelve pieces of flair at soul-sucking corporate chains. And I'd watched many a ma and pa burn their businesses, life savings, and marriages to the ground. But despite the discomfort of having to live these experiences, I'd learned so much from each. I had learned how to run a restaurant by first witnessing what *not* to do. And failure is a *visceral* instructor. It reveals every mistake. Every flaw. Every oversight. And with my face so intimately familiarized with the floor, I gained the confidence that I could divert myself from the same fate. I had seen the industry's pitfalls. Its circular dance of repeated missteps. I knew its warts. And I felt prepared to do something different. I was ready to start a company of my own. The question was *how to get started.*

Rather than focus on *how* to start a company, I focused on *who* to start a company with. I'd seen various owners operate in a vacuum of familiar faces with questionable opinions and zero relevant experience. Their inner circle, typically composed entirely of close friends and relatives, often completely lacked firsthand knowledge. And it had cost them. In an industry that creates so much strain on the humans working within it, I wanted somebody to help ease the burden. I was determined to find someone who complemented me, and I them. I wanted to work with someone with whom I wouldn't mind spending the countless hours of collaboration that would inevitably be needed for the company to be successful. And my future partner would need to *believe* in our combined potential as much as I did. For I had no money. And there would be no guarantees.

This was a good time for self-reflection. To meditate on my personal abilities and desires. A time to admit which restaurant responsibilities would drown me in a pool of my own tears. And it was a time to consider who it was that could best cover my ass. I needed to admit what it was that I did and did not know.

My years in consulting taught me how to *run* restaurants. I knew ops like I knew my own toes. I was more than proficient at hiring a team and creating a culture and operating service and making guests happy. But I didn't know how to physically construct restaurants. In fact, I knew jack shit about construction. I'd never been to a city department to pull a permit. I'd never picked a paint color or worked with an architect or overseen a general contractor. I didn't know a damn thing about raising money. Or writing a deal. Or signing a commercial lease. Never had I created a brand. Some things I knew I could learn. Others, well, I just wanted to find someone who was already good at it. And who would be equally happy to avoid the work that *I* was good at. I wanted to find someone with vastly different skills but the same goals. The same passion. Dedication. Persistence. Shit . . . Somebody who would say yes . . .

I first met Holly Fox at a two-story Italian restaurant that I recall as being very large and very red and, despite its Ferrari styling, very slow. I'd been working as a restaurant operations consultant, and Holly, an employee of the restaurant's management group, had been tasked with determining if the red racer could be revived. At only twenty-four, she was fulfilling a role typically reserved for people born a generation before. Warm, observably sharp, and meticulously organized, Holly had an edge that made one wisely consider one's words before speaking. And she seemed to eat work for breakfast. I was excited to attempt a resurrection together. But our proposal was declined, and the red restaurant eventually closed. Our first chance to work together had been snuffed out. By Holly.

There would be more false starts. Years after first meeting, Holly and I were surprised to find each other as new hires for a quickly growing restaurant group. But quickly growing quickly became quickly sinking, and the entire company imploded. That was our second chance to collaborate, extinguished in less than three months. But three months in restaurants is like three years in the normal world. And during this time, I'd learned that Holly had grown up in California's Palm Springs area. And that her family had been running local grocery stores for decades. That she'd been learning about wine since grade school. And that she'd adopted a slightly psychotic dog that required anxiety medication. And she had her sister's birthday tattooed in black ink on her forearm. And she operated a candle company as a side hustle. Holly had been *building* restaurants. Overseeing everything from interior design to permitting to construction to branding and all the little stuff in between. And she loved restaurants as much as I did.

My mind was set. I prepared to make Holly an offer that would officially forge our alliance. But I'd never written a "deal" and was oblivious about how they existed in the world of business. So, I would keep things stupidly standard. Stupid, in this case, a *good* thing. I would propose that we split the company down the middle. Like a business-form black-and-white cookie. And that's about all I had to offer. There would be no contracts to sign. And I could guarantee no salaries or wages. There would be no benefits for the foreseeable future. There was even the possibility of *losing* money at some point. And there was more than a distinct possibility that we could lose a *lot* of time. So, given the circumstances, offering half of a spoken-word agreement felt like the only proposal Holly might realistically shake on.

To set the scene appropriately, I asked Holly to meet in a neon-lit, day-drinking Hollywood dive bar. The same dive bar that had served as our gossip nest while watching the previously mentioned company wither and die. It was a place of pure nostalgia for us both. And in the middle of the afternoon at the Frolic Room, with '80s heavy metal blasting from the jukebox, I made my pitch. I asked Holly to start a restaurant company. A restaurant *consulting* company. She had lots of questions. I had few answers. But as the day turned to night, and with Holly's objectivity absolutely altered by the unrivaled confidence of a boozy afternoon, she raised a glass.

"Fuck it!" she said. "Let's start a company! What if we call it Last Word Hospitality?"

I raised my glass to hers, grinning like a seal, and knocked back a shot. "Last Word *Hospitality*?" The Frolic Room was not a place I'd be seen ordering our new namesake cocktail, and I tried not to puke warm tequila, proposing, "Why not Last Word *Restaurants*?"

"Adam! Do you have a secret plan and secret investor and secret space for us to open our own spot?" Holly was daintily covering her mouth with two hands and blinking like a fairy.

"Touché, Holly Fox. Touché. Last Word *Hospitality* we shall be."

And that was that. Our partnership forged with a toast in place of signatures. Witnessed only by day-drinking patrons in studded, heavy leather. We had no formal structure or strategy whatsoever. No paperwork. No funding. No location. Just a couple of bozos at the bar getting into business. However! We "owned" a company. A consulting company. We had nothing to lose and so much to gain. What those gains would be, we had not a clue. But that didn't matter. We were going to choose our own path. Destination to be determined. And it felt positively *grand*.

Make It Official

To build a partnership on stable ground, that ground should be clearly defined from the very start. And the best way to clearly define the conditions of any partnership is through an official company document known as an "operating agreement." An OA is essentially a platonic marriage contract and a prenuptial agreement rolled into one. It outlines who owns what, who's responsible for what, what happens if the company takes off, and what happens if the opposite occurs. It will serve as your company's central document. Your guiding light. It may cost you a few bucks and some tedious legwork with an attorney (admittedly, it took Holly and me over a year to save up enough dough to have one drafted), but the simple act of putting together the damn thing makes it that much less likely you'll ever need to use it. Consider it your very own personal constitution.

Revenue Isn't the Only Growth That Matters

Holly and I would spend the next three years growing our company like an oak tree. Often imperceptibly, and not without an occasional branch snapping off. Each new sprout was hard earned. Germinated through blood, sweat, and *time.* But growth had not been our priority. Far from it. For the first few years, the primary objective of Last Word was simply to *survive.* For to survive was to succeed.

And while fighting to keep our heads above water, Holly and I began the process of turning Last Word into a real-life company. We'd started with incremental infrastructure investments. Mostly little stuff. Business cards, a website, and other budget-friendly, official-appearing swag. But we kept no office. We hired no staff. And our clean bill of expenses allowed for a regular, albeit limited, flow of funds to be deposited into a legal-fee cookie jar. Saving up for those *official* Last Word Hospitality company documents I told you about. For at this point, Last Word was about as official as a lemonade stand. And lawyers would cost quite a bit more than lemons.

Now, despite the less than glamorous realities of our consulting practice, Holly and I were soccer-mom proud that Last Word was officially operating. But pride itself doesn't pay the rent. And our earnings had never matched what we'd been making in our previous gigs. In fact, Holly was still working a full-time gig—with Last Word as a full-time side hustle—while I chased down client after client after client. Often for nothing. What we did have was a secondary, *secret* source of income. *We were learning.* A valuable form of compensation that no amount of money can replace. We were learning how to find clients and how to serve them. And in the process, learning how to create a restaurant of our own.

We'd created a pretty little deck. Nothing more impressive than a high school book report, really, and we began to outline the ways in which we could help restaurants. We could create comprehensive business plans. Hone concepts. Scout locations. Oversee the permitting and construction process. Provide technically basic, but ultra-creative design services. Recruit a team. Train that team. Build a menu. And then bring it all together. Essentially, we could *make* restaurants. And when we looked at the list we'd created, we felt pretty damn good that Last Word Hospitality was a company worth hiring.

And what had begun with one contract, a key referral from one of my previous employers, led to another. And that one, to another. And so on. *We were making friends.* Doing good business led to more business. Being easy to work with led to easy leads. Creating relationships that would turn out to be immensely important in the future of Last Word. And as our earnings stabilized across multiple clients, we crossed the first *major* hurtle we'd faced as a company. *Financial independence.* Holly quit her job. We were finally, and *truly*, self-employed.

This may sound odd, but Holly and I had been quite fortunate to struggle so early, and so often, in our company's history.

Our partnership had been tested from the very beginning. We had stuck together when things went bad. And things had often gone bad. And we had stuck together when money was tight. And money was always tight. We'd assumed mutual responsibility for every success. And for every failure. Our confidence, like roots into soil, was growing by the day. But we knew that our continued existence depended entirely on planting our efforts in the right patch of sunshine.

So, we decided to strike out to explore new pastures. With some semblance of stability beneath us, we felt prepared to take new risks. To work towards new dreams. And to apply all that we had learned as consultants into our own attempt as restaurant creators. We started talking about our own place—a little neighborhood oyster bar.

The Last Word "Model"

If building a restaurant from the ground up had once appeared a distant mirage, it was now something like a landscape photograph. Ansel Adams–like in its clarity. While many of our clients focused on developing the *concept* of their restaurant, which is how a restaurant appears to diners, we concentrated on developing the *model* of our future place. The model was the sketch hidden beneath an oil painting. The functionality behind the form. We would create an intimate, welcoming place. Timeless. But innovative. It would follow old traditions, while blazing its own. Holly and I had evolved an idea of how a restaurant could operate in a novel, genuinely old-school, but pioneering way. Rather than seeking "concepts" we'd seek *people.* And rather than building dreams, we'd build a new reality.

And no, that didn't mean lab-grown oysters, surge pricing, or robot bartenders. You see, since time immortal, or at least since I started working in restaurants, staff has been organized in the style of the *brigade.* A stuffy, timeworn, Frenchy, militaristic system for organizing staff. The brigade structure splits the team in half into back of house, or BOH, and front of house, or FOH. Kitchen and dining room—*may they never mix.* Well, we were going to smash those boundaries to smithereens.

Holly and I believed that the rigidity of the traditional brigade made for segregated, and boring, workplaces. And not only was this separate and unequal approach a big bummer, it was also inefficient. "That's not my job" is the most divisive utterance in all of restaurants. And the more specialized each role in the restaurant became, the more likely one was to hear it. We wanted to blend the two sides into one team. We would create a crew of oyster-shucking bartenders who would steal the show. Technical, but personable. Producers, but sellers. One team, instead of two. And Found Oyster would be their proving ground.

Always Celebrate the Beginning

There is no greater small victory than deciding to start something with someone else. Especially something as difficult to navigate as a small business. And although you may just be getting started, and you may wish to be further ahead on your voyage, the creation of a partnership is always worth celebrating. It means that you'll have somebody to bounce ideas off of. Someone trying to accomplish the same goals as you. Someone willing to take the same risks. Someone to have your back when shit goes sideways. It means that somebody believes in you. And at the end of a very long day, maybe even a day when nothing went right, when your ideas didn't work out, when everything sucked, or when you lost, you won't be alone. And if that's not worth celebrating, well, let's just say there will be plenty of days to write off. Enjoy the good days.

· 4 ·

The Long, Uncomfortable Road to Funding (Part 1)

Holly and I were seated on the "patio" of a coffee shop in a shopping mall. Carved out of the indoor plaza's main thoroughfare, it provided the privacy of an airport terminal. Across the Formica table from us sat Nick. Nick was *apparently* a successful business dude who had *supposedly* invested in a few local restaurants. He wore a crisp, white, short-sleeved shirt, tucked into crisp, white khakis, and had crisp, white hair. He was a shark in the shape of a human. I had hoped to host the meeting at the LWH office, but Nick had insisted we meet for coffee. At 5 PM. On a Friday. At the mall.

"Hi Nick, thanks for taking the time to meet with us. We've been hearing about your support for restaurants, behind the scenes it seems, and we're honored to have your ear." I attempted to portray champagne confidence, which I most certainly did not feel. "Did you have a chance to look through the deck we sent over?" Holly and I were very proud of our deck.

Nick appeared to be looking for the bathroom as he replied, "I'm sorry, guys. But honestly, I never got around to it. But I will tell you, I've heard great things about you both. Really great. It's a poke bowl concept you're working on, right? I think your email said it was a poke bowl concept. Really, really smart. They seem to be popping up everywhere. Easy to run and limited up-front capital requirements, I hear. Really smart. I do wonder what happens if the price of tuna shoots up?"

A fucking poke shop?! I let out a nervous laugh and hoped we could navigate this early storm of miscommunication. After months of active fundraising, every meeting still felt like a swim in an algae bloom. It was awkward, presenting something we'd been working on for half a decade to a total stranger. Then asking for investment in a *theoretical* restaurant. And as we dove into a fluorescent-green pool of concept explanations and neighborhood descriptions and self-justification, reaching the other side felt a long, long way off.

"Well, we are doing a *seafood* restaurant, Nick. On Fountain, in East Hollywood. But, *ah*, we're opening an *oyster* bar. Not a *poke* shop. Not that I don't love poke. But we're trying to do something a bit more, well . . . *personal*."

I could tell from Nick's eyebrows that he thought this was a stupid thing to say. "Well, guys, I know you have a lot of experience, but I do have a few immediate concerns. I don't totally get why you're fixated on an oyster bar. Not everybody loves those salty little boogers, *amiright*? Why not roll with a proven concept? Everybody loves Italian food. Steak. Burgers. In this city, tacos. Why *oysters*?"

Nick, like most potential investors, remained fixated on the *concept* of Found Oyster. And his feelings about the concept, also like those of most potential investors, mirrored his feelings about seafood. When investors loved seafood, they loved the concept. If they hated seafood, they hated the concept. Worst yet were shellfish allergies. I've yet to find an investor who puts money into something that gives them hives. Of course, a huge reason why *we* were invested in the concept was because of the integrated staffing model of Found Oyster. And so I, like I had many times before, tried to steer the conversation back to the functionality of our vision.

"Listen, Nick. You're right. Not everybody loves oysters. But people who love oysters *love oysters*. East Hollywood has a *ton* of great restaurants. But nothing like this. It's smack-dab in the middle of the city, and this idea we have about oyster-shucking bartenders is a big deal. It's hyperefficient *and* guests are going to love it."

"No, I get it. Don't get me wrong, guys—oysters might not be my thing, but I get it." Nick massaged an invisible beard as he went on. "Now, let me ask you this: When me and my buddies go out to dinner, we like Catch in West Hollywood. Usually, it's like four or five of us dudes. I'd say we drop like two or three grand on an average dinner . . . *Easily*. Maybe more if my pal Keith is choosing the wine. Guy thinks he's a connoisseur. Anyways, that place is *packed* every fuckin' night. How do you think Found compares to Catch?"

The winds of warped expectations continued to blow. Catch was a well-funded, and massive, NYC transplant restaurant. We're talking about enough seats for a Baldwin family reunion. It was situated on a luxury building's rooftop in an affluent neighborhood with a retractable roof. Found would not be like Catch. And though it was tempting to compare the two—as projecting Catch-like financials would have made fundraising easier—setting realistic expectations was central to avoiding drama down the line.

Healthy numbers, we could do. Catch numbers, we could not. "Success" needed to be defined from the very start.

Feeling the ship lurch downward, I sensed there wasn't much to lose. And with the sideways smirk of a captain who had made his peace, I said, "Well, Nick, Found really won't be anything like Catch. Honestly, man, not at all. Catch is a behemoth. Found will be a little baby minnow. But we can create Catch-like *energy* with far fewer people. And for a lot, *lot* less investment. LA needs something like this. I'm telling you, Nick. Found Oyster is going to be a neighborhood *institution*."

Nick paused and continued to stroke his nonexistent beard. He seemed to be searching for bullshit deep within my retinas. Then he said, "An *institution*, you say? Well, shit, Adam. That doesn't sound too bad!" Nick turned to Holly. "What do you think, Holly? Is your partner right, or is he fuckin' nuts?"

"Most certainly both," Holly said with a straight face. "And I can tell you this, Nick. People are going to be talking about Found Oyster. And if you'd like to join us, we can celebrate your investment at Catch."

Nick let out a genuine belly laugh that would win over any skeptic of his character. "OK! OK! I'll bring the boys and we'll burn the fucking house down. Email me the prospectus and I'll go through it tonight. You guys make me want to spend money!"

It was a great way to end a meeting. And it was the last we ever heard from Nick the Shark.

"No. Nope. No thanks.
Not now. Not ever. No way."

Don't be surprised if you experience a wide variety of rejection. "No," apparently, is the onion of words—there are layers upon layers of ways to say no. And even the stodgiest of investors may display boundless creativity when telling you to take a hike. You may be ghosted. Have meetings canceled last minute. Some people will say your concept is too niche. The neighborhood too unknown. Your experience, inadequate. Some potential investors won't like the name. Some will think you're raising too much money. Others will think you're raising too little. The restaurant is going to be too small. Your dreams, too big. And other, *safer*, investments need to take precedence. The kids need piano lessons. *No.*

> There is no avoiding rejection. So, wear each one like a battle scar. Learn to learn from getting told to get lost. And with each "no," search for little things that may lead the next potential investor to say "yes." You'll need to get out there and stay out there until you get what you need. It may not be fun, but to make a restaurant, you're most certainly going to need the money. So, go get it.

Cooking Up a Deal

As you may have noticed, restaurant investments have a bad reputation. And as such, raising money for Found Oyster would mean starting in a hole that we didn't dig. Now, in a typical pitch, I would dance around discussing "the deal" until a potential investor had been reasonably swooned. But with you, dear, sweet reader, I shall begin with the meat and potatoes. Later, we'll talk about the sauce. You see, deep within every meeting, every pitch, and every presentation, there was a financial *commitment* required to move forward. And to make that commitment, investors needed to believe in something other than the viability of Found Oyster, the restaurant, which didn't exist yet. They needed to believe in Found Oyster, *the opportunity.*

Holly and I had only written one deal before. And the "I get half, you get half, and we're both in charge" approach we'd adopted with Last Word was not going to work for Found Oyster. I researched restaurant deals and found no real standard. Somehow, we needed to determine how investments would be structured, what shares would be worth, how many shares we would sell. Most importantly, we needed to establish how we would maintain control. All of these individual elements are what is known as the "mechanics" of a deal. And having never apprenticed in an investing shop of any kind, we were forced to design our investment vessel by learning on the fly.

These deal mechanics were then delivered to our legal counsel who turned them into, you guessed it, more paperwork. Another operating agreement was produced. And to outline investment terms, another document known as a "subscription agreement." I shan't bore you with the details. Mostly because I have no idea what they are. An example, the first of many, of hiring experts in areas where you are not one.

What I do know is the broad strokes of how the deal was structured. There would be three categories of partners, each known as a "class." First were to be cash investors, known as "limited partners." They would have zero responsibilities and zero control.

Next were the "operating partners," the chef and general manager. Their equity would be earned through *time*, with no cash investment required. They would oversee the day-to-day operations of Found Oyster and receive full salaries.

The third class would be the "general partners" or GPs. That would be Last Word. We would be in control, receive a "management fee" calculated as a percentage of sales, and act as the "fiduciaries" of the restaurant. Which is to say, we would have a legal responsibility to make decisions in the best interest of the business and provide ongoing updates to the other partners.

We then needed to determine how much equity each class was to receive for their contribution to the restaurant. How to slice the pie? Well, while there are trained finance bros in sharkskin suits who employ countless methods to structure these types of deals, if I've learned one thing about making *deal* pie, it's that a simple pie is a better pie. And it would be far easier to sell a good old-fashioned peach cobbler investment than some newfangled concoction cooked up with a banker's recipe. The key ingredient, for me at least, is *fairness*.

Alternative Funding. And Hindsight.

Now you may be asking, "Why not just go to a bank and borrow money?" Well, that's because banks are *terrified* of restaurants. When a bank loans money, it does so with the understanding that if the business can't pay, it will take possession of that business and sell off its assets. But here's the thing about restaurant "assets." Their resale value is next to nil. And that makes bankers very, *very* nervous. They don't want to be repossessing tables and chairs and napkins and cases of onions and turned fish. If we had owned the real estate, that would be a different story. If we were financing a generational restaurant with a marathon track record, that would be a different story. If we had huge personal wealth and could leverage other assets to get a loan, well, that would have been freaking great. But we had none of those things. The closest we got to securing a bank loan was a credit card.

But, if by some Hollywood miracle a time-traveling DeLorean were to show up at my door, I might jump in with Doc and Marty and implement a few *small* changes to the Found Oyster deal. And those changes, although considerably less valuable than placing bets on sports matches whose outcomes were certain, would have increased our percentage of ownership. This could have been accomplished by introducing a "preferred return" to the mechanics of the deal. A preferred return, or a "pref," is a deal in which cash investors accept *less equity* in a business in return for a *significantly higher* portion of profits in the short run. Once paid back in full, known as "being made whole," the terms would flip. "The flip" being the moment that cash starts being distributed by actual ownership. Thus, delivering a larger piece of the pie, in the long term, for those who do restaurant work.

Anyway. You know what they say about hindsight in the restaurant business.

Fuhgeddaboudit, dood!

The Prospectus: A Paper Lighthouse

To sell our deal, we needed to clearly present the recipe we'd be following to turn 4880 Fountain Ave into Found Oyster and Found Oyster into a profitable business. We did so by creating a prospectus—essentially a fancier sounding term for business plan. *This was the sauce.* Meant to dress the meat and potatoes with a more colorful composition. It was a conversational can opener, a tool to bypass the initial awkwardness of asking for money, a mouthwatering slideshow to provide an overview of the project and efficiently move past the "what the hell is this?" phase. Better to cross that bridge before sitting down for coffee at the mall.

And in creating the prospectus for Found Oyster, we included a combination of imagery and information that exhibited the overall cohesion of our project. It will *look* like this, *feel* like this, and *operate* like this. We showcased how this restaurant would be different from its peers. And most importantly, we tried to show that Found Oyster was a unique investment opportunity. An opportunity that would provide a positive financial and *social* impact on their lives.

You see, unlike stocks or bonds or securities, restaurant investments provide an *experience* like no other. Focusing on the *model* of Found Oyster, which Holly and I were so proud of, proved inadequate in motivating investors to take the risk. The financial proposition alone was just not enough to bring investors to the table. But no matter how much money they invested in Apple, nobody was going to recognize them at the Genius Bar. Investing in Found Oyster, on the other hand, meant being *part* of Found Oyster. The staff would know their name. The chef would send them special snacks when they came in. And we hoped that the magic that attracts guests to dine in restaurants had the same effect on investors. They could *live* this investment. And we needed to bring that feeling to life. On paper.

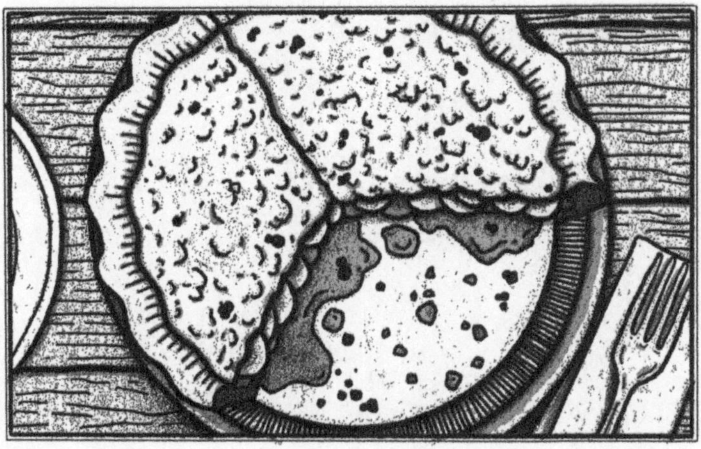

A Pie of a Partnership

Baking a partnership pie can be as complicated or as simple as you'd like. A deal is like a ball of dough. You can shape it and stretch it into a wide variety of shapes and sizes. You can fill it with fruit or custard or meringue or even meat. But remember, the more complicated and intricate the layers and the more exotic the ingredients, the more likely people will question your methods. The further you stray from a classic, the less certainty you'll have on how things will turn out. But the more you work with the dough, the more you'll understand it. You'll start to *feel* what *feels right*. So, start with simple shapes. Simple fillings. Simple ideas materialized as simple pies. Pies of partnership. You'll know you got it right when everyone at the table is satiated with their piece.

• 5 •

The Long, Uncomfortable Road to Funding (Part 2)

Last Word had signed its largest, and most questionable, consulting contract. A soup-to-nuts development project, we would be assisting a heavily trust-funded, heavily opinionated, minimally experienced son of a British furniture magnate open the restaurant of his dreams. In transparency, Holly and I hoped that by helping this fortunate son accomplish his goals, maybe he'd consider a significant investment in ours. On one of Beverly Hills' chicest streets, standing before an Olympic-swimming-pool-sized, uncertified, preowned, enormously expensive restaurant, our client, Mr. H we shall call him, explained his "vision":

> The restaurants in this city are absolute *shit*. Like, there are only three or four spots in the whole city that would matter in London or New York. *Michelin* barely even steps foot in this town. And no restaurants with three stars? In a city of this size? It's a fucking joke. I'm telling you guys, it's total *shit*.

Looking back, I now see that our hope for big fat investment had been doomed from the start. Holly and I were never able to satisfy Mr. H's demands as a client, not to mention as an investor. What eventually caused this great divide was an antithesis of beliefs. What I believed were many great restaurants in Los Angeles—restaurants worth investigating and understanding as a way of understanding the city—Mr. H believed were beneath the international standard of what a *great* restaurant must be.

But if there was anything that I was *sure* of when it came to judging a restaurant, it's that *everybody's* opinion is different. And LA is sure as shit not London. Mr. H felt otherwise. As our relationship turned sour, Holly's and my dream of a single source for funding went out with the tide.

And with a modus operandi for burning bridges to the ground, the last thing I ever heard from Mr. H, before he hung up on me that is, was, "I'm not fucking paying you, Adam! You and Holly have no idea what you're doing and, frankly, I'm sick of it. Your services are no longer required. *Nobody* tells me how to spend *my* fucking money."

Click.

Now, there is a common myth that a single high-net-worth individual is needed to open a restaurant. Opportunities often languish while hopeful operators lie in wait like Ahab for this mystical white whale. While there were certainly leviathans out there in the investor sea, we never found one. And from our experiences working with furniture-magnate-inheritor types, and others like him, we had learned that there were two types of investors—not big or small but *good* or *bad*.

We could have a beer with good investors. *Publicly.* Not so for a bad investor. And as quickly and as often as *we* were rejected, we, too, moved on quickly and often from investors that raised red flags. And those red flags needn't be the obvious symptoms of bullies or bullshitters. There were financial red flags to consider. We needed investors whose bets were within the realm of what they could afford to lose. Now, nobody wants to lose money. This is true of people at all levels of income. And even a great friend may turn into a sworn enemy if money lost was money that needed not to be lost. Frantic calls from spouses demanding the return of their investment, already spent on tables, chairs, mixing bowls, and other nonrefundable items, were well worth avoiding. When it comes to fishing for investors, you need to know which is a keeper and which should be thrown back to the sea.

When to Toe the Line. And When to Draw a New One.

You will have people question your deal. And you'll need to be prepared to explain your reasoning. There will be people who'll ask you to *change* your deal. And you'll need to be prepared to tell them why you won't. There are moments when you'll need to stand tall and defend your position.

Sometimes that will lead to investors dropping out. So be it. Not everyone will be charmed by you. Such is life.

Although we found no whales while raking the ocean for financial supporters, some people do. And whales will expect the ocean to part on their behalf. They may want to change the terms in exchange for a single, significant, project-moving investment. And I won't mince words: A single funding source is a massive advantage. But the leverage of these leviathans is quite different from that of minnows. And if you do indeed find yourself swimming with a whale, *be cautious*. There are more considerations than money when choosing a major partner. Can they advise you? Do they know restaurants? Do they have other connections, be it vendors, media, real estate folks, contractors, etc., that will help fuel your business? How are you feeling about sitting down for that beer at your favorite bar? If you're going to change your deal for one person, that person should be just as appealing as their investment.

A Pool of Little Fishies

Fundraising for Found Oyster was like surfing a cresting, budgetary wave that we dared not turn back to see. It would take Holly and me the entire process of building Found Oyster to fund Found Oyster. These were *parallel* tracks. While Holly was in construction meetings, I was meeting with potential investors. When she was pulling building permits, I was meeting with potential investors. And when Holly was picking paint colors and chairs and plateware and art, I was meeting with potential investors. There was never a time while we were building the restaurant that we weren't also trying to fund it.

As you might imagine by now, raising funds for Found Oyster never ceased being a slog. But nothing advanced our goals like showing potential investors the space in *real life*. Bellying up to the *actual* bar, or at least, where the bar *would* be. Maybe sipping on wine while donning a hard hat. And the more 4880 Fountain Ave looked like Found Oyster, the lighter our tread through the fundraising bog.

We talked to *dozens of* potential investors. Formally. We sent decks to and had light conversations with dozens and dozens and dozens more. And while it may sound like a numbers game, it wasn't. It was a *relationship* game. As we progressed through person after person and meeting after meeting, what became obvious was the foundational reason for each person's investment. It wasn't the location that closed the deal. It wasn't the concept. Nor was it the model. It wasn't pretty pictures of oysters. And it wasn't the prospectus. It was *us*. One investor after another would let it slip in some form or another: "I don't know shit about restaurants, but I know the two of *you*. And I'll take a wager that Adam Weisblatt and Holly Fox figure this out." It was the most human kind of bet.

And one by one, intermittently, and sandwiched between rejections, we started to find investors. And slowly, in an ocean of refusals we began to find believers willing to say that most beautiful of words: *Yes*.

IIIIIIII

We'd started our fundraising mission where most people do: with *family*. And yes, the stories you've heard are true. Doing business with kin has the potential for generational disaster. So, to do commerce with our own blood and brood, while protecting our familial relationships, we pitched the restaurant like we would to any prospective investor. We provided complete presentations. We explained the prospectus in full, patient detail. Financials were discussed with the same seriousness we would have shown a sovereign wealth fund. If they called with questions, we picked up the phone.

Next, we moved on to friends. Among those friends we found plenty of willing investors. But the extent of investment we were asking for left many of our biggest supporters on the sidelines. Soon, we set out upon a deep-sea fishing expedition of drinks with acquaintances, semi-cold calls, meetings in malls, and "reunions" with former roommates' ex-boyfriends, when, almost by accident, Holly and I identified a group that would become most of Found's patron saints: *previous clients*.

Our previous consulting clients had seen our restaurant aptitudes firsthand, often in challenging circumstances. And if consulting had proven to be a frustrating, stutter-step business, it was all forgiven when we realized the network it had left us with. This group was accustomed to taking risks on restaurants. And it was from within this pool of contacts that we began to pull fish out of the sea. Little fish, but keepers all the same.

After a hot streak, we fell into a slump. Our early momentum had fallen to the wayside, and we found ourselves back in the dire straits of a rejection river. The final shares, weighing us down like a two-ton anchor. And as we checked off name after name after name in our lifelong network, crossing off every social media "friend," every former coworker, and every neighbor, the feeling of futility started to creep into our reality. We went in search of a new route.

There's More Than One Way to Filet a Fish

Long before cash or coins or credit cards, there was bartering. Old-fashioned and transparent by its very nature. Trade used to mean exactly that—I give you this thing for that thing, and we both get something we want. Holly and I now turned to this most ancient of customs in our attempt to overcome the barrier before us. And so, it was back through the piles of folded jeans, paper goods, and mountains of citrus that we once again sat down with Moses. We had a trade in mind. I had a feeling that Moses would be down for a good old-fashioned exchange of something for something.

And for once, I was right. Moses loved it. And a negotiation that began with updates on each of our respective families ended with a deal. Our second with Moses. He would pay for half of his share in cash. The other half, in abated rent. Our collective interests, now soundly residing in the same boat. And while Holly and I were in a bartering mood, we identified another natural partner who may have interest in a trade.

Holly and I had first met Jake Burns while working for a mutual client. Jake had been the general contractor, and we had been operations consultants. And although that project, which will remain unnamed, was another saga in our great book of misadventures, Holly liked working with Jake and suggested we choose him to build Found Oyster. This was a big moment, for a good relationship with a builder can be as productive as it is *relieving*. Jake had constructed dozens of restaurants, but he had never been given the opportunity to maintain a connection with something he'd helped create. And we had a feeling that Jake would be willing to turn a few of his chips into dice. Jake would forgo much of his fee in exchange for equity in the restaurant. His eloquent response, at long, long last, closed our fundraising journey.

"Oh, hell yeah. Let it roll, guys. I'm fucking *in*!"

IIIIIIII

And now we return to the topic of parallel tracks, for there was another, equally vital process taking place while we were fundraising and building the restaurant. *We started looking for operating partners*. And with a lifetime of restaurant friends between us, we found them. Soon, the Found Oyster core would expand. A general manager and a chef were joining the team. And together, we would be bringing the restaurant to life—maybe sooner, and in a different form, than any of us expected.

Juggling Is Required

I'd love to tell you that opening a restaurant is a linear achievement. A process that starts in one place and ends in another. But very much like restaurant service, building a restaurant requires you to coordinate multiple objectives on multiple timelines. Fundraising and development are often happening simultaneously. And you may be tossed from side to side in the stormy seas of getting things done. But to accomplish something as complicated as making a restaurant, you'll need to trust yourself. You'll need to believe that you'll get the job done *no matter what*. That even if it takes fifty balls to the head before you master the art of juggling, you will learn to juggle. Because sometimes, all you can do is throw a few tasks in the air and do your damn best to catch them.

·6·

Restaurants Are *Human* Stories

There was once a tostada. A shimmering, tongue-tickling scallop tostada with fennel, cilantro, and apple. Stacked tall like a Roman column, the ingredients dressed in a bright green sauce of summer. People loved the tostada. Holly loved the tostada. I loved the tostada. And then one day, it was gone.

This tostada had been the star of our surprise Found Oyster "pop-up" series. And when I say *surprise*, I mean it surprised *us* as much as anybody else. Hosted on the patio of a friend's wine bar, we'd launched the new series to promote the restaurant and generate early interest. At least that was the message we were projecting. In truth, we were worried about running out of money. And if it sounds like we were always worried about money, that's because we were, most certainly, *always* worried about money. It's not an unusual sentiment during a restaurant opening.

Shocked by the removal of such a delicious tostada from the pop-up menu, I went in search of answers. And I demanded Joe Laraja, soon to be Found Oyster's first general manager, explain this brash development.

"I don't know, dude!" Joe responded with his shoulders up to his ears. "Everybody loved the last one. But you know, Ari made a new one. And I think it's better! It's insane, really. That guy is the real deal, my friend."

A tall, handsome, mostly bald fella, Joe wore his standard attire: an oyster farm T-shirt and a *different* oyster farm's baseball cap. A fellow Bay Stater transplant, Joe tended to attribute table numbers to Boston athletes: "Ah, that lobster roll is going to Larry Bird. *You don't know?* That's table thirty-three." His was the exact kind of edgy but warm, and sometimes wisecracking, personality we wanted Found Oyster to be known for.

"Alright. Well, shit," I muttered. "I loved the old one. We're serving the new one today?"

"Yeah, man. Don't worry about it. I'm telling ya, it's fire."

"Joe, you know what they say about shit that ain't broke—"

"*Yeah, yeah, yeah.* Sit down for a minute, will ya? You're distracting me, *dood*. I need to finish setting up."

"*Ya, ya, ya . . .*"

Almost never dressed in chef's whites, Ari Kolender arrived in tan linen pants, a black linen shirt, and latticed brown leather shoes. His hair, a tangle of curls paired with a short goatee. More dapper professor than cook, Ari was not the kind of chef to sport a toque, nor a chef's coat with his name emblazoned on his chest. He thrived in a dining room as much as the kitchen—a hugely important dynamic in the future of Found Oyster.

"What up, y'all? Adam, you workin' today or hanging?"

"Most certainly hanging. And what's this I hear about you fucking with a new classic? After just two pop-ups? What's up with that?"

"Hold on there, guy!" Ari chuckled. "Y'all haven't tasted the new one yet. Let Joe and me get set up and we'll have you hooked."

"Alright, alright. You know, I loved that tostada—"

"Just give us a second, will ya? Get a glass of wine and chill for a minute."

"Alright, alright."

Ari was already operating his own restaurant across town, Hayden, but had agreed to create the Found Oyster menu and mentor a young chef. A young chef whom we were yet to identify. A native Charlestonian who'd maintained remnants of a southern drawl, always more pronounced when drinking or charming guests, Ari had one of the calmest demeanors I'd encountered in a chef. But despite this outward tranquility, the man could flat-out *cook*. And he shucked oysters like an otter with a black belt.

Guests began to arrive, and a line snaked across the patio. At its head, Joe and Ari were taking orders, shucking oysters, plating tostadas, filling lobster rolls, and entertaining the crowd like a couple of seafood-taming Siegfried and Roys. *It was beautiful.* Rounds of people were receiving their orders. They were smiling and laughing and slurping oysters and gulping wine. Holly and I smiled at each other. Found Oyster was getting closer by the day.

Soon, Holly and I joined the back of the line. When we reached the front, we greeted the guys like any customer would. And after playing through the niceties of a typical restaurant transaction, Ari handed us the new tostada. To which I responded, in true Masshole form, "A *new* tostada, ya say, *dood*? Bettah be one *wicked* fuckin tostada, *kehd*."

"You guys want to hear about it, or not?" Ari paused, his eyebrows high. "Alright, then. It's a fried corn tortilla, topped with sliced scallops, grated apple, yuzu kosho, and purple basil. And I'm *sure* y'all are going to love this one more than the last version."

"Well, we'll be *sure* to let you guys know," Holly said with a dry smile. Everyone knew that Holly's opinion would be, well, unvarnished.

Now, dear reader, I must admit, *taste* is a very hard thing to judge. And, like music, one person's preference is sure to be another's torture. But for me at least it took but a single bite of this tostada to reach a new and thrilling realization. Found Oyster was going to be *special*. And Ari had the potential to stock our menu with far more intriguing offerings than well-executed lobster rolls and properly shucked oysters. I looked at Holly and saw that same epiphany simultaneously occurring in her mind. The first tostada had been amazing. The second was *magic*. It was going to be a beloved dish at Found Oyster. Ari and Joe had been right. And I could feel a wave building beneath us.

Meet the Main Characters

The best restaurants, just like the best movies and books, are true stories. Not true in a factual, *Encyclopedia Britannica* kind of way, but "true" in a Cohen brothers "it's true that it's a story" kind of way. For Found Oyster to feel true, it needed to share a central story about *what* it was serving, *why* it was serving what it served, and *who* would be serving it. Found Oyster had the sketch of an operational and ideological framework, but there were nearly endless opportunities to be creative as the restaurant came together. From recipes to service style to uniforms, Joe and Ari would now join as co-creators of Found Oyster. Their truths were now our truths. And we would need to integrate our various plotlines into a central narrative. A single story born from many stories.

Joe

Joe was born and raised in a small town on Cape Cod. His dad, a local attorney, was the kind of guy who ate the same lunch at the same restaurant every day. That restaurant, aptly named Land Ho!, was where Joe spent his childhood, a place where servers and bartenders knew who he was and what grade he was in. When I first met him, he had been working as a server in one of LA's best and busiest restaurants, and we became fast friends talking about Massachusetts and reminiscing over Massachusetts and generally being Massachusettsans. Now, I don't say "Masshole," because Joe is not a Masshole. The Cape often produces a different breed of kinder, gentler folk. And Joe is a true product of Cape Cod.

Although Joe had no actual management experience, I believed fully in his potential. Maybe not to run *any* restaurant, but specifically to run Found Oyster. Joe understood the soul of the restaurant we wanted to bring to LA. And when compared to Joe's current place of employment, Found Oyster would have fit in the walk-in. But there was an even deeper connection between Joe Laraja, the person, and Found Oyster, the restaurant. You see, not only could Joe slay oysters with the best of them, *he grew them*. The Laraja family operated an oyster farm in the small cape town of Orleans. This was a potential piece of the Found Oyster story that would be very difficult to replicate.

And so Holly and I offered Joe the opportunity to join Found Oyster as its general manager. And as a partner. *And* as our primary source of oysters. But he was hesitant. Not one to dive in without testing the waters, Joe had plenty of concerns. This would be Joe's first time assuming the responsibility of a restaurant, and he'd been in the business long enough to know that responsibility meant it would be *his* phone ringing in the middle of date night. Joe was not naïve about how frequently those calls could occur, or what disasters might await on the other end of the line. And he was reluctant to accept equity as part of his compensation.

Sitting at a rickety coffee table on the sidewalk near Found Oyster, I found myself negotiating equity percentages with Joe. Or rather, Joe was negotiating *out* of an ownership percentage. He crossed his arms and tapped his elbows while he jostled his way into not being an owner. "What if I *didn't* accept any equity and, in exchange, we could boost my salary up a bit?"

"Well, buddy," I responded, "I understand where you're coming from. But that's not how we're looking at this position. We want a *partner* in the room at all times."

"Yeah. But what if the restaurant doesn't make any money?"

"If the restaurant doesn't make any money, we're all in trouble."

"Good point."

"Joe, I think that time will show that getting a piece of Found Oyster will be a financially and *emotionally* rewarding experience. I don't want to talk you into *anything*, but I *do* want to talk you into *this*. I want you to take the equity."

"Well, what if I split my equity in half and take half in salary boost?"

"If that's what you really want to do, I'm open to it. But before you make up your mind, I think you should call your dad."

Now, I am not privy to the finer points discussed between Joe and his dad that day, but soon after they discussed the opportunity, Joe accepted our offer. If I were to speculate, I imagine that two major points swayed Joe's decision. The first was obvious to any attorney reviewing the terms of the deal. Equity is hard to get and rarely offered without being asked for. The second reason did not appear on paper but was probably more important (I certainly thought it was more important). You see, the Laraja family was bonded around this oyster farm. It had been Joe's older brother Mike's oyster farm. Mike passed away tragically. And the family took over the farm. They worked it together. They grieved through it. They healed through it. And those Little Namskaket oysters, as they are known, would be the restaurant's unofficially official bivalve—an ongoing tribute to Mike Laraja.

Ari

Ari's path into restaurants closely resembled my own. Meaning, he followed an unglamorous and bumpy road. Ari had started cooking when he was young. He worked in some bad restaurants, went to some unaccredited, probably fraudulent culinary school, and finally started working in good restaurants where he committed another decade of his life while rising to the coveted title of "chef." The title mostly led to fourteen-hour days with lunch consumed over a trash can, but like most cooks, the title was preferred over no title.

Unlike the raw talent we saw in Joe, Ari had an accomplished highlight reel of running kitchens. He had been nominated for prestigious awards and highlighted on "important" platforms. He had played a pivotal role in the launch of Charleston's The Ordinary, then as the opening executive chef at Leon's Fine Poultry and Oysters, where he had served entire armadas of properly shucked bivalves and fried chicken to the joyful masses. But Ari's accolades were far less impressive, to me at least, than what he was doing at his current restaurant, Hayden. You see, Hayden was not built to be a restaurant. It was a cold, concrete, glass, and steel retail space more appropriate for showcasing lingerie or laptops than serving food. And within this fish tank of a restaurant, Ari was preparing an entire menu, three meals a day, with what might as well have been a camping setup. He had a handful of electric burners, an electric oven, a row of waffle irons, and an electric toaster—that was it.

So, beginning one's day with his waffles, topped with white miso plums that sang like Sting, or to lunch upon his roasted eggplant with whipped feta popping off the plate like Bonnie Raitt, or to enjoy a dinner of braised pork shoulder with lima bean pistou shredding like B. B. King butter, was to understand that Ari knew how to do very much—with very little. And it was exactly this type of galley-style organization and resourceful cooking that gave us faith that Ari was particularly well suited to create the food at Found Oyster.

A *Personal* Advantage

There is something special about knowing the owner of a restaurant. One feels differently when dining in a place with which they have a personal connection. The food just tastes a little better. And the seats are a bit more comfortable. And the energy of the room is more intimate. More important. And more irresistible. Even when the check is dropped, the blow is softened by the feeling of one's hard-earned cash staying in the family. And *this* is your biggest advantage. Especially over your corporate peers. Your restaurant can feel human. And theirs can't.

But to create this sensation, even when you're not in the room, you'll need to incorporate the personalities, talent, and passion of your team. A restaurant is just an empty box until human beings bring it to life.

> And while you most certainly want to imprint yourself deeply into the DNA of your restaurant, building a personal connection with a broader range of your crew will change what it feels like to work there. And to dine there. You need your team to feel as connected to the restaurant as you do. If the restaurant becomes theirs as much as it's yours, they'll feel it. And care for it. And your guests will feel it. And they'll return for it.

The Final Share

After months of working together, Ari had asked Holly and me to meet him behind the kitchen at Hayden. And there we stood, like a buncha wannabe spy dweebs, about to discuss a failure that would directly impact Found Oyster's chances of success. "Hey y'all, thanks for coming by," Ari said. "I have some pretty shitty news for you guys. Hayden is closing."

"Oh, fuck! I'm sorry, man." I sympathized. "Tough business, restaurants are. You doing alright? The crew know yet?"

"Yeah, man. We just told everybody this morning. My partners are going to take the space in a different direction. Which means . . ."

"Which means you need a job." I shuffled my feet, attempting to conceal my excitement.

"Which means I need a job."

I looked at Holly. She squinted and delicately nodded her head up and down. "Alright, man. Well, I'm bummed to hear about Hayden. But, as you *very well know*, we're opening a little oyster bar in East Hollywood." I noticed Ari trying to suppress the corner of a smile. "Give Holly and me a couple of days and we'll come up with something official for you to consider. I don't think I'm speaking out of turn when I say we'd really like to have you as a more permanent fixture at Found Oyster . . ." Ari was beaming. And so was Holly. And yes, of course, so was I.

Now, I could rattle off about half a dozen clichés about one door closing and another opening. But let's just say I don't mind blowing off the hinges from time to time. Ari had become a friend. He and Joe got along real swell. He had run oyster bars before. Good ones. Holly and I decided to dive deeper into the pool. We carved additional shares out of our own ownership stake and made what we thought was a generous offer. And that offer was accepted. With it, Ari was now fully committed as the chef and general partner of Found Oyster. And Found Oyster was inching ever closer to existence.

Sweat Means Success

Offering someone a job is a nice feeling. But offering them a piece of ownership is another feeling entirely. It feels *fantastic*. We all want to be owners. And introducing your team as partners will have everybody puffing their chests with pride. But before patting yourself on the back for being such a swell pal, remember that exchanging equity for sweat is exactly that—an exchange. You won't be parting with anything, for owning "more" of a failing restaurant is not a good thing. Restaurants are only valuable if they're successful. And restaurants *need* people to be successful. This is a human investment. Not altruism. This is good business. And that's OK. In a world that typically rewards those with the most cash, prioritizing talent in restaurants is what leads to success. Success, and longevity. Longevity and, might I say, yet again, *love*.

• 7 •

A Concept of Cohesion

Joe and I were sitting at the bar of a corporate boardroom of a restaurant. The stools beneath us were upholstered with faux leather and large enough for the ass of an elephant. We were enjoying fried calamari with pickled peppers and gin martinis with blue-cheese-stuffed olives. This was to be our first stop of many on a trail of inspiration.

"I don't know, man. I mean, isn't *this* what *most* people want? Big comfy seats. TVs with the game. Pro service. Properly fried calamari." Joe popped a crispy tentacle in his mouth. "*I* certainly love places like this. And I think they're pretty damn good at doing what they do."

"You're not wrong," I responded. "I mean, this calamari is, indeed, crispy and delicious. And this is a damn good martini. And my ass is very, very well accounted for. But would you want to come here every day?"

"No."

"Why?"

"You know why, man. I really *like* it here. The food is great. And consistent. And the service is great. And consistent. But it just . . . It isn't special . . ."

"I agree. It's missing that *thing.* Whatever that thing is. I just don't think you can make a restaurant, copy it like a floppy disk, and drop it wherever you want. Not while retaining that thing that made it special in the first place." I sat back in the grand stool. "And I sure as shit don't feel like it's *only us* having this experience. We could be sitting in a Sephora."

"Totally, man. We could be anywhere. None of this feels like LA. And my dad? He'd never come here! Dick Laraja needs a place to feel like it's been there for decades or he just can't trust them. By the way, where do these places get *so many hunting scenes*? Like, is it somebody's job to just comb the country for oil paintings of horses? It's crazy, right?!"

I swallowed the last of my martini, ate my blue-cheese-stuffed olive, and responded, "I think you're right, Joe. Let's ask if they've got a nautical source for Found."

"Now you're thinking, man. Now you're thinking."

Joe and I spent that evening discussing the many things we wanted Found Oyster to be known for. Descriptors that we hoped to hear from our guests. And descriptors that we would be proud of if the folks back home heard about the restaurant. We wanted to be known as a neighborhood joint, but one worth traveling for. We wanted to be egalitarian, but elevated. Approachable, but exciting. Simple, but well-sourced. Nostalgic, but creating new memories. It would be a delicate dance. For Found Oyster to stand the test of time, it would need to integrate itself into the patchwork of a city teeming with restaurants. And our primary goal was to make it seem like Found had been there all along. A little slice of the Land Ho! But in LA.

And as the project inched ever closer to launch, I felt that it was time to visit the Mecca of oyster-shucking prowess. Joe knew it well. Holly had been multiple times. I had gone on every occasion it was physically possible. But Ari had not been. It was time to pay our respects to the kings of the shuck. But, of course, we had no budget for even the most enviable of frivolities. So, with plane tickets out of the question, we decided to drive. Our destination: two couches at my sister-in-law Bevan's apartment.

We would not be going to Cape Cod but to San Francisco.

Now, I would be a big fat phony liar if I did not disclose my love of this institutional San Francisco restaurant. Swan Oyster Depot has been serving up fresh oysters, crab cocktail, clam chowder, and crudo since it first arose as the *Titanic* went down. Guests queue up for a seat. Barstools only. Breakfast and lunch only. Seafood only. An old San Francisco place where the rules is the rules and you must follow those rules to be rewarded. Or don't follow the rules and be removed. Your bartender takes your order, shucks your oysters, plates your crudo, and acts as a singular guide through a land of succulent raw seafood.

Ari and I would spend an entire morning eating enough for a legion of walruses—a truly inspiring experience while we molded Found Oyster into what we hoped would be our own segment in the great saga of restaurants.

The Intangibles of Identity

Swan Oyster Depot was not the only restaurant we visited, discussed, or studied. But it did represent the style of restaurant on which the four of us had become fixated. These restaurants did not share a common owner, cuisine, or concept. What they *did* share was longevity. We wanted to know what it was about old restaurants that had allowed them to grow, well, *old*. In a business that famously kills in youth, every city or town that still maintains independent operators has at least one restaurant that is decades older than the rest. How does a restaurant become an *institution*?

Consistency was the first thing we noticed. Regardless of one's opinions on the quality of what was being served at these dinosaur establishments, each long-serving spot we visited served their same product, in the same way, every day, to every customer. And that consistency came across as *honesty*. These places could be trusted. They stayed true to who they were. And they made no false claims about what one could expect from them. But consistency is something that companies like McCheeseGarden are very, very good at. So, what was different? What was that *thing*?

Next, we noticed that institutional restaurants had developed their own style over many years, even decades. Accumulating art, tchotchkes, recipes, personalities, regulars, and memories until evolving into whatever *it* is. Swan Oyster Depot isn't like anywhere else. Every detail within Swan feels cohesive. The style of the food is connected to the style of service. Which is connected to the style of barstools. Which connects to the music being played. Which connects to the taste of crab fat spread across sourdough. A tale told through five senses. And although inspired by our ancestors, we hoped that one day, Found Oyster would simply be like Found Oyster and nowhere else.

Honesty Leads to History

A restaurant is an *interconnected place.* A place in which every decision affects the decision that follows. And as your *dream* of a restaurant turns into a *physical* restaurant, you'll need to find a central theme to guide each small choice. Each small choice, contributing in one way or another to the cohesiveness of the restaurant you are to create. Each small choice, combining into the *identity* of the restaurant that you'll introduce to the world. A lot of those choices, will, indeed, *finally* be about *food.*

And while it's easy to make proclamations about the food your restaurant is going to serve, it's more difficult to make those proclamations true. Cooking is *hard*, ingredients, inconsistent, and the more people you're cooking for, the harder it gets. Even the simplest dish may become a Gordon Ramsay nightmare if the right steps aren't taken ahead of time. So before making promises, you need to be damn sure you can keep them. For what you *want* to do—and what you're *capable* of doing—aren't always the same thing. *Acceptance is key.* And if you can be honest with *yourself,* you'll vastly improve your chances of building the kind of trust that places like Swan Oyster Depot took decades to build. Your own contribution, one dish at a time, to the big book of restaurant history.

Cuisine-Based Dialogue

The food at Found Oyster would be, and needed to be, uniquely Ari's. But the process of developing the menu was, and needed to be, collaborative. Ari was not creating *any* oyster bar menu, and he was not simply creating *his* menu. Ari was creating his interpretation of what a New England oyster bar in Los Angeles should have on its menu. The Found Oyster menu.

R&D would take place in our home kitchens—with one significant caveat. Home kitchens are not restaurant kitchens. And everything that Ari cooked, and the rest of us tasted, would need to once again be cooked, tested, and tasted when we finally accessed the Found Oyster facilities. Those facilities were still an empty shell.

Our "development sessions" tended to steer into dinner-party territory. Spouses and friends often attended, and various bottles of wine were often opened, "tested," and *never* spat. So, to maintain some semblance of form and direction for the process, we created a "wire frame"—a simple outline that communicated the general balance of the menu. It would keep us on track while working through lobster rolls and appropriate wine pairings.

First, we workshopped the chowder. Now, I have consumed hundreds of varieties of New England clam chowder in my day. Maybe thousands. And like most Massholes, I felt Cam Neely–confident in my ability to differentiate between any and all forms of our regional, clam-flavored, cream-and-flour soup. But where I once believed that a spoon should stand like King Arthur's sword in a properly made cup, Ari's version wouldn't have steadied a straw. But it was buttery, and silky, and filled with potatoes and clams that miraculously retained their texture. And what suddenly became so exciting wasn't a menu mimicking a Cape Cod oyster shack but a clam shack with the creativity of an unburdened chef at its helm. Maybe it was because he'd never been to New England, but Ari was naturally free from doing things the "old way." He would do things "his way." It was the only way he knew how.

And with each tasting, the menu began coming together. Spinach-artichoke dip spun off into salt cod–artichoke dip, which was then named "cheesy artichoke brandade with fresh tortilla chips." "Chicken-fried" oysters were accompanied by an umami-juiced sake lees mayo. The lobster "bisque" roll explained itself. And hints of Ari's Charlestonian roots began appearing throughout the menu. First, through various usages of Old Bay. Then Ari made his own "New Bay." Peel-and-eat prawns came with suitably named "special sauce." The Found Oyster wedge salad would appear at tables as a hulking iceberg of iceberg smothered with blue cheese and smoky bacon and tomato. Perfectly chilled and unapologetically classic. And you've already heard my thoughts on Ari's tostada.

But even if it was Ari cooking all the food the rest of us were tasting, there was a distinct advantage to experiencing and discussing each dish through a collective palate. Each partner's preferences, or lack thereof, played a role in understanding how a wider audience would receive each offering. Each partner would view each dish through a different lens, as would our future guests. What was most important wasn't getting Ari *correct* feedback, it was about providing *honest* feedback. Because "spicy" is never a fact.

Joe would typically be the first to speak. And what he would say was often the most predictable. You see, Joe had, and has, a brotastic crush on everything Ari cooks. His comments, delivered directly after devouring, often sounded something like, "Whoa, I mean . . . It's fucking *delicious*. Maybe throw a little Crystal Hot Sauce on there? See ya later . . ."

Holly, predictable only in that her answers would be murderously candid, would often speak second. "*Yum*. I really like the texture of the fish. Super delicious. It does leave me wanting a little something fatty to rich it up. Just a little bit of sluttiness. Salt is perfect. Seasoning perfect. Maybe just a little extra smut . . ."

My own responses mostly fixated on the dish as a product that we would *sell*. "I'm with Holly. I mean, who couldn't use a little extra smut in their lives? How much would we be charging for it? Maybe the dish gets a whimsical, oceanic name of some kind? Like we'd name a cocktail. We could call it Poseidon's—"

Holly was cupping her cheek and shaking her head: "*What?!*"

Since inception, we'd envisioned Found Oyster as a clam shack—no frills, plain and simple, good seafood. But it had become clear that Ari's creativity expanded beyond what a lobster roll would ever need. And while we remained committed to evoking the *feeling* of its New England ancestors, none of us wanted to limit Ari to a Legal Sea Foods selection of dishes. If it tasted delicious, we wanted it on the menu. For we also knew that even a nostalgic New Englander would not crave lobster rolls every day. And we knew that Angelenos would not consume fried seafood at the same rate as Bostonians. The menu would highlight the hits. But it would also afford space to any dish, flavor, or ingredient that Ari felt would go nicely next to an ice-cold canned beer. Or wine! We would sell lots of wine!

If you're wondering why *cocktails* weren't part of the plan, the answer is quite simple: We couldn't afford the license. *That's it.*

Creativity with Intention

As you engage in the wholly enjoyable process of making a restaurant menu, remember that just because something is "new" doesn't mean it's good. And creativity for the sake of creativity usually leads to a big steaming pile of crap. But to feel something new in an experience that isn't new, to be surprised by something familiar, *that* is where the art of making a restaurant lies. It's in telling the story of a cheeseburger, but differently. It's about creating a neighborhood noodle shop that somehow feels fresh. The steak house, but personal. A classic diner, but different. The city's 233rd Italian restaurant, but, well, better. You shouldn't be afraid to put your take on whatever you damn well please when making a restaurant. But don't throw marshmallows on pizza and tell people it's new. Nobody cares. *Identity* is the great guide of restaurant innovation.

Addition by Subtraction

This may sound odd to my non-Masshole readers, but I'd always dreamed of bringing roast beef sandwiches to Los Angeles. Not just *any* roast beef sandwiches, of course. Roast beef sandwiches in the style of the North Shore of Massachusetts. A region where one's preferred "beef" could cause a bottle-smashing riot at the pub. It had been a passion of mine since moving to California to share the secular pleasures of a "three way" with my new community. That is, thinly sliced, medium-rare roast beef. Tangy BBQ sauce. Mayo. And cheese. All layered in a big pile on a big fat fluffy onion roll. Found Oyster was going to be my opportunity to share this delicacy with a new generation of three-way hedonists and homesick Massholes.

Ari was perplexed. "Like an Arby's sandwich?" he asked.

"No! Not like an Arby's sandwich, Ari. Mass style. Like a Harrison's Roast Beef sandwich. Or Nick's. Like fucking Zeno's! Not like Arby's."

"OK. So, are all these spots roasting their own beef?"

"I assume so? I see them slicing the meat and making sandwiches. I'm not sure where the beef is coming from. What are you getting at?"

"Well, buddy. It may be difficult to *roast* our own beef. Seeing as we don't have an oven."

"Right."

"So, to serve these sandwiches, we'd be sourcing a precooked roast beef product of some kind. And we'd need to establish an entire station in the kitchen to slice the beef and make the sandwiches. And we'd be devoting an equally important section of the fridge for backup precooked roast beef product. But! At least we'll be ready to serve 'beef' sandwiches with mayonnaise, BBQ sauce, and American cheese. Nothing at all like Arby's, of course."

"Of course."

After allowing me a few days to process the potential end of yet another lifelong dream, Ari suggested we offer a steak off the grill as our token offering of beef. A workingman's cut from a local ranch with house-made hôtel butter. Fresh herbs. Lemon. Black pepper. Simple. Delicious. And realistic. I concurred at first taste.

One day, I will bring "three ways" to California. But I had to let go of the idea of it happening at Found.

And yet, "the beef" was not the last of my ideas to be defeated by better ideas. Especially regarding the menu. Originally, I had imagined Found Oyster offering a rotating selection of six or seven oysters. When in season, the Little Namskakets would take center stage. The supporting cast would include oysters from around the Northeast, the Pacific Northwest, California's coast, and maybe an occasional variety from Japan. This approach was not new. Offering a wide variety of oysters had become a trademark standard for most restaurants dedicated to bivalves. But Joe and Ari wanted to cap our selection at two.

Sacrilege! I thought. *Blasphemy!* First the roast beef sandwiches, and now this! Oyster lovers must have choices! They needed variety! The spice of life! Why in the holy hell would we only serve two types of oysters?

But per usual, there was a sane, totally reasonable rationale behind Joe and Ari's decision to drive me to madness. We would only serve two types of oysters so we would only be serving *great* oysters. Less variety meant less chances for an inferior product. The boys explained that the more oysters we carried, the more likely the bottom of the list would be, well, the bottom of the list. These oysters would be *different*, sure. But does different matter when it's different for the worse? Joe asked me a very simple question: "Adam, dude, when have you ever seen a selection of oysters at any of the historic spots back home?"

The answer was never. The old-school spots sold "oysters." Location assumed to be local. And that was that. Found Oyster would carry no more than two oysters at a time. Great ones only.

The Business of a Menu

If building flavor is about balancing sweet and salty and bitter and spicy and umami, then value is built upon something far more complicated. Taste is most certainly impacted by cultural perspective, but value is based *entirely* upon it. You see, Found Oyster's offering would be judged by far more than its plated appearance or deliciousness. Some foods have a culturally high perception of value. Caviar. Lobster. Filet mignon. Truffles. And some foods have a culturally low perception of value. Bread. Ground beef. Lettuce. Catfish. But the effort that goes into preparing each of these items in a restaurant is often at odds with these preconceived notions. Bread takes a night and day and a lot of work and a lot of love and a lot of equipment and a lot of space and a lot of people to make and serve. Caviar takes a spoon.

And so, in the same way Ari went about balancing the flavors of each dish, we would balance the entire menu. And not just by mixing tastes and textures, but in the effort required to assemble each dish and the price we would pass on to our guests. To further explain Found's menu pricing, a bespectacled economist may refer to our method as "elastic." Elastic, meaning pricing would stretch from affordable to extravagant, with items existing all along the spectrum. And we hoped this pliability of pricing would create variability of visitation—grabbing a beer and a chowder with some pals after work; impressing the in-laws with a jaw-dropping raw bar platter; longtime lovers reignited over oyster after oyster; or a bartender stopping in after work in desperate need of a nightcap. We craved a mix of customers—mostly in small groups, celebrating or commiserating. We wanted to create a menu that catered to the ups and downs and wins and losses of daily life. And you know what? It makes me want to write poetry.

A Verse on Taste and Value

Everything tastes different at the beach.
Or in a cafeteria.
Or after a long hike.
Or while stuck in traffic.
Or lounging on a scenic veranda.
Or under fluorescent lighting.

Or from a fine glass.
Or from an old mug.
Or drank from a plastic cup.
Or when the sun is shining.
Or the wind is blowing.
Or while walking through a vineyard.
Or presented by a suited server.
Or at the ball game.
Or with elbows resting on a well-worn bar.
Or while in love.
Or in mourning.
Value, too, is determined by the senses.
Sight. Touch. Scent. Sound. And yes. Taste.
Each adds or detracts. Consciously or not. Invisible or not.
In everlasting marriage. Taste and value.
Because a lobster roll is never just a lobster roll.
Even when it's just a lobster roll.

·8·

Designing a Pretty Machine

Holly was standing with one leopard-print shoe buried in a pile of pulverized white sand, the other cat foot perched upon a shard of smashed concrete. She was facing the newly revealed innards of Found Oyster. And against what remained of a mangled wall, she dramatized her new idea, delicately delivering a platter of imaginary oysters to Mr. and Mrs. Casper.

"Imagine an oyster stand attached to the wall. A server would approach with the platter, pull the stand down like a lever. *Like so.* And place the tray on top," she said, stepping back and projecting a theatrical palm at the beautiful functionality of her idea.

"Like an oyster Murphy bed?" I asked.

"Like an *oyster Murphy bed*? Adam? What?"

"Who doesn't love a Murphy bed?! I lived on a Murphy bed for a year when I was living down in—*What?*"

Holly leered at me with glazed eyes.

"OK, *heard*, Holly Fox. I like the oyster *'stands.'*" I made sure to bend two peace signs for emphasis.

"Good. Because it will save a few precious centimeters of table space for actual plates and glasses, they'll be cheap to build, and—" I returned the double-doughnut stare. "You know what, never mind. We need to catch up with Jake."

And standing in the middle of Found Oyster with a puzzled look on his face, straddling a tributary of plumbing trench, was

Jake. As you know, Jake was our general contractor and now, a partner. A SoCal native who looked the part, Jake was a tattooed, restaurant-building surfer who didn't surf. Anyway, he had this habit of making video task lists on his phone while he paced around the site. Back and forth he would go. Pointing at shit and talking to himself.

"OK. So Holly wants to install the levered oyster stands over each table. Here, here, and here. The bathroom gets demoed. Plumbing connects to the sewer line here. Gas, here. The bar will run lengthwise along this wall. Refrigeration below. Stainless-steel counter above. Millwork shelving above that. One row of tables along this opposite wall. Booths on either side of the front door, if they can even keep this storefront. It's gonna be close."

A passerby may have thought Jake was batshit. But they'd be wrong. Jake is a creative builder who has a system. And crazy as that system may have appeared, it worked. But the news continued to dampen our hopes of preserving the original storefront. Replacing it would require we design, engineer, and build an entirely new façade. And a wider front door would eliminate the space we needed for booths on either side of the entrance. Front window booths would, no doubt, be the best seats in the house. If we got unlucky, the total number of booths at Found Oyster would be cut in half. From two to one.

After completing his self-made, instructional reality show, Jake was ready to roll. "OK, guys. First of all, I just want to thank both of you for choosing us on this project. Thank you, Holly. Thank you, Adam. I can't tell you how much it means to me to be a part of something like this." He took a moment to look us both in the eye. Jake was old-school in that way. We liked that Jake was old-school. "Anyway it's going to be a tight fit for, well, a tight fit for everything, really. We're ready to go when you guys are. When did you want to get started?"

Construction was fully in Holly's domain. "As close to now as possible."

"Ha! OK, sure. I can get my guys over here to demo early next week. Then we'll start layering in the trades. I do have some bad news, though. You guys aren't gonna like it."

"Go ahead." Holly tilted her head like a predatory bird.

"I think the storefront's gonna have to go. We don't have the clearance, and the only other way to get it would be to shorten the bar. Which I assume, and suggest, as your partner, we don't do. There just aren't a lot of options."

Jake had a nonchalant way of handling new challenges. He was perpetually calm and doggedly sought realistic solutions. And he never complained. These were highly desirable traits to find in a general contractor (GC). Or in any partner, for that matter. You see, there are physical realities to building a restaurant that don't reveal themselves when you're dreaming about a restaurant. And as it turns out, there are realities to building a restaurant that don't reveal themselves while *planning* a restaurant, either. But Jake and Holly developed a rapport that kept creativity flowing and the project rolling, often saving us from the very expensive activity of indecision.

"And don't we also lose a booth if we lose the storefront?" Holly asked, gently kicking a wayward screw through the dirt.

Knowing When to Let Go

Critical sacrifice is the mechanism that brings restaurants to life. And deciding when to let go, and when to hold on for dear life, means constantly reevaluating what's most important. In a tight space, on a tight budget, these decisions happen in real time. Sometimes, you'll get to spend money on things you want. Other times, you'll be spending money on things you'd hoped to avoid. But forward you'll lurch. Pipe by pipe. Frame by frame. Hazard by hazard. Every decision impacting how your restaurant will meet the world. And while there's no limit to the limitations that following a budget may create, it's often all the things you *can't* afford that drive a distinct sense of punk-rock ingenuity. A punk-rock ingenuity that guests will *feel* when they sit in a place that you've bled for.

"You do. Now, I'm not saying there is no chance this doorway doesn't get approved. It is possible that they let it slip." Jake measured once again to confirm. "You're about half an inch short. It's up to you, but I wouldn't risk it. We can engage on the new storefront immediately. Or, we let it ride. It's your choice."

"That sounds like a dangerous gamble to take, Jake." Holly turned to me. "Adam, you ready for this?"

"*Ah, fuck*. Well, doesn't sound like we have much of a choice."

"No. No, we do not. OK, Jake, let's get going on a new storefront. I don't want to get screwed down the line because we're feeling sentimental," Holly said.

"Yes, ma'am." Jake nodded and walked away to make a movie about destroying my favorite part of the restaurant.

Goodbye, sweet booth. You were almost the best seat in the house.

First, a Skeleton

Moving forward we would encounter three distinct phases of development: to design, permit, and build Found Oyster. Each presenting its own opportunities for creativity. And for shit to go catastrophically wrong. We would need to navigate all three phases—while balancing our timelines and budget—to create a restaurant with the *cohesive* identity we strived to create. And the next few months would determine how closely Found Oyster, the restaurant, resembled Found Oyster, the dream.

Restaurant design is based upon the functionality of a single space for multiple purposes. An art form in predicting human movement, comfort, and collisions. And even the slightest miscalculation can act as a fish bone in the throat of even the best-laid plans. Things fit or they don't. And with space to work within limited to that of a Boston Whaler, accounting for every item in our inventory, every piece of equipment, every shucker, every server, and every diner would require carefully considered centimeters.

But rather than ogle a paper floor plan for hours, trying to navigate the room in a procession of stick-figure synchronization, we played a physical version of pretend restaurant. We used blue painter's tape to indicate the location of tables, chairs, equipment, and so on. And we ran dozens of restaurant-themed simulations acting like guests or like staff—ordering food, shucking oysters, waiting tables, waiting for a table, or waiting for someone to finish in the bathroom. We tested equipment layouts, floor plans, and seating arrangements. Acting our way through efficiencies and stopgaps and bottlenecks and fender-bender-inducing blind corners.

Standing in one of those blind corners in a barren Found Oyster, I continued my habit of apparently staring into space. Which I suppose I was. But on the inside, I allowed a childlike sense of wonder to play out in my mind. I allowed myself to *feel* a room full of people and personalities. Reaching out into the ether to experience the packing of guests and staff and lots of stuff into this tin of sardines. And then orchestrating all the little fishies into a *Swan Lake* of shucking knives, alcohol, and fire—

"*Adam* . . . Hello in there? You want to take a look at this?"

Holly jolted me back to present day, East Hollywood. "Huh? Oh, yes! Yes. Sorry, I was just thinking about something."

"You were thinking about something, alright."

The floor of 4880 Fountain Ave now looked like a geometric kindergarten project. From it we sketched a crayon-quality floor plan. But these scribblings were not to be judged by their obvious lack of drafting talent. Rather than waiting for an architect to create plans from scratch, *we* had established the fundamental layout of Found Oyster. And by delivering even the simplest drawings of the restaurant ahead of time, our desired workflows would be drafted into our first set of plans. For, if we were to create the oyster-shucking rock stars we'd been promising, the stage would need to be set just right.

And upon a splintering folding table, Holly pushed aside a large pack of bottled water, one of those blue tins of cookies from somewhere Scandinavian, and a couple of packages of instant ramen, and laid out our first set of architectural plans. A mandatory part of our process, only an architect could draw official plans deemed acceptable by the many agencies little Found Oyster would need to be approved by. And although many architects provide *design* services, our almighty budget forced a less glamorous route. We would pay for bare-bones architecture, equipment engineering, and assistance with city submissions. There would be no presentations on materiality.

No design narratives. And no 3D renderings. We had a basic floor plan and our imaginations.

Now, imagine for a moment, just as we were imagining, the wondrous complexity held within a single page of *Where's Waldo*. That was the type of depth we wanted to create in Found Oyster. What were basic blueprints were for us but a canvas. A setting to mix the many tiny details of a restaurant into a mosaic of story and discovery. Lots of little things all adding up to one larger thing. But there would be no mahogany in Found Oyster. No copper light fixtures. No handmade wallpaper. No items of beauty that only money can buy. The complexity of character within the restaurant would need to be created, or acquired, on the cheap. And so began a process of repurposing and reimagining anything and everything that would enrich the identity of the restaurant.

A timeless checkerboard floor was composed of heavily discounted tiles from discontinued lines. Our soaring backbar, the focal point of the entire restaurant, a plywood masterpiece. The *new* storefront, shamefully shiny compared to its antiqued ancestor, was made of affordable aluminum. But warmed by a well-worn, Faulkner-aged front door, it regained much of its old-world charm. The door, being the only part of the façade that guests would often *touch*, was one of most expensive items Holly sourced for the restaurant. When guests were expected to physically interact with something, we tried to use pleasingly *real* materials. If decidedly out of reach, we stuck to movie-set façades.

Then, Skin

Once we had established the skeletal structure of Found Oyster, we could begin to apply the *skin*. Or, to continue my lame, book-length obsession with sea-based synonyms, the *scales*. The scales of the restaurant were comprised of everything that guests would *feel*, *see*, *hear*, *taste*, and *touch*. And with no sense neglected, the design process would include the selection of everything from barstools to subwoofers. Light fixtures to menu paper. Flatware to signage. And without a design team, each individual piece would need to be selected by us. Each item balanced into a natural sense of *belonging*. And belonging begins with the sensation of having been there before . . .

We wanted Found Oyster to feel like it had stood there for decades. People would walk by and wonder how they'd never noticed the cute little restaurant sitting right there. A lived-in place. Well worn. Beat down a little bit. Blue collar and comfortable and inviting like Cape Cod. Romantic and chic and exhilarating like Los Angeles. A place that felt like home while transporting you elsewhere. A place where you would wonder what the walls would say if they could talk. We wanted to design a new restaurant that looked and felt like an old restaurant. A restaurant that people would simply want to be in. And although we could not force the true patina of age, some of it could be found.

"*Look out, y'all!*" A ghoulish fish head came barreling around the corner of a grandma's china cabinet, which was filled with blue-and-white ceramics. Holly screamed her fucking head off.

"What the fuck! Ari! You scared the shit out of me!"

"Well, technically it wasn't me. It was our new parrotfish friend here."

"That thing is the size of a fucking poodle."

"What do you think? Found Oyster mascot?" Ari raised an eyebrow, modeling the monster fish like Vanna White.

Holly answered, "I think, no."

The three of us were antiquing in an old antique shop that smelled like antiqued kitty litter. And it was from this gymnasium-sized Parthenon of old junk, and others like it, that the soul of Found Oyster would be sourced. Now, despite the torture Ari was inflicting upon Holly with Polly the Poltergeist Parrotfish, our mission was clearly defined. We were looking for serviceware, decor, and art. But not the kind of art found in museums, galleries, or fancy folks' homes. Our search was for the art of the tchotchke.

"Hey guys, come over here for a minute," I said.

"What ya got, big guy?" Ari replaced the big fish on a chimneyless mantel and walked over to my box of gleaming stuff.

"It's somebody's old collection of ice cream bowls. And each is marked from a different hotel across the state. I mean, look at this. The del Coronado. Chateau Marmont. These are old. Shit, this one is from the Cecil! Maybe they're fucking haunted."

Each dish was as heavy as a grapefruit and made of the classic silver-appearing material once found in fine hotels all across the land, *silver plate.*

Ari picked up a bowl and rotated it in his hand. "Yeah, man, these are great. We can use them for smaller oyster platters or something. Super cool. You think somebody collected all of these?"

"Oh, definitely. And whoever it was stole each and every one. I bet they were ordering room service, enjoying their sundae draped in hotel bathrobes, then a quick rinse in the bathroom sink, and into the luggage. A little keepsake for the kids back home."

"I love 'em."

"Me too. And they're cheap. Let's buy all of it."

And we did. And this was just the beginning. On we went, raiding anything cheap and Found Oyster-y like a thrifty Indiana Jones. We acquired every ornamented oyster fork in the city. A defunct hotel's entire stock of plates. A Japanese fish trap, to be hung from the ceiling, transformed into contemporary art. An antique wine bottle opener made from sturdy West German steel attached to the bar like a medieval torture device. It spouted bottles and spat corks for breakfast, lunch, and dinner. And we scoured the seven antique seas for any and all forms of silver plate, acquiring trunk loads of the shiny serviceware last used under Nixon to be recommissioned for everything from check presenters to oyster trays. Supposedly dated, heavily discounted, and physically immortal, this much maligned vessel would become a signature at the restaurant.

While it was tempting to fill Found Oyster to the brim with cheeky nostalgia, it was equally vital to leave things behind. We thought it wise to skip Boston sports memorabilia. Our intention was to share the *heart* of New England, not the knuckles. We would limit, but not totally ignore, buoys, lobster traps, anchors, and fishing tackle. And if we were to hang pieces of maritime memorabilia, we did so with finesse. There would be no TVs. No Keno. No fluorescent lighting. Compared to the seafood joints I grew up with, Found Oyster would be more dimly lit and warmed by our endless commitment to candlelight. The art more dramatic and varied. The colors more—well, I should probably say something about the seemingly simple subject of picking out paint colors.

Choosing paint colors for a restaurant is hard. Really hard. Surprisingly hard. And I, Adam Weisblatt, fully capable of dressing myself in the morning, was completely and utterly helpless when it came to weighing in on a permanent palette for the restaurant. Picking my daily getup was one thing, but deciding upon a color scheme to wear year after year without trying it on first—well, I just couldn't help. Poor Holly got no feedback from me. When the paint first went up at Found Oyster, I think she almost cracked in half. Holly hated it. I wouldn't have used such strong language, but it didn't seem quite right. While we'd never had the budget nor inclination to hire a designer, we needed help. And specialized help we did find. Holly hired a color consultant. It was an expense that bought more than a pretty palette of color. It was an investment in Holly's sanity.

Don't Be Afraid to Ask for Help

It's hard to ask for help. Especially when that help costs money. But, if you're going to survive the process of building a restaurant, you'll need plenty of hands. And to assuage your concerns about spending extra money on what may be perceived as a human luxury, remember this: *The initial cost of specialists can be misleading.* And while it's true that the additional fees of additional help may appear as a red stain upon your pre-opening budget, when you need help—and there are times when we, all of us, need help—it's likely to create a cost savings rather than an additional expense in the end. So, get help before you *need* help. From attorneys to designers to architects to CPAs, building an outside team is a key part of the process. And should you ever feel like an amateur because you're seeking counsel elsewhere, know that the opposite is true. Being a professional means knowing what you don't know. Seek assistance. Be proud. Move forward.

• 9 •

Permits. More Permits. And Construction.

Did you have fun in that last chapter, dear, sweet reader? Oh, I bet you did. *Everybody* loves the design portion of making a restaurant. *Everybody* loves picking glassware and barstools and running their fingers along various wood grains for the bar. And *everybody* loves imagining diners living and laughing and loving in their future restaurant. Well, enough of that. Let's dig into the shit. And don't you dare skip it, you permit-avoiding plate picker, you! For if Found Oyster were to live, it would require many a blessing by the powers that be.

Unfortunately, the path to permitting a restaurant is often as clear as a Cheech and Chong storyline. And in all the scrolls of antiquity there would be inadequate space for the boundless rules, regulations, codes, requirements, and standards that we would need to adhere to in the building of our little restaurant. We were now in the business of rule following. Or, at least *attempting* to be rule followers. Many of the rules we encountered were rainy-day gray. And as we sailed our dinghy that was Found Oyster through a torrent of bureaucracy, we tried not to get lost in the oncoming storm. But rather than bore you to a death by a million permits, I shall instead share a single story.

And so, without further ado, "A Tale of Two Addresses."

The day began like any other day, or at least any day while in the midst of a restaurant opening. Ejecting from bed and into a brimming pot of coffee, I began to comb through the forty-six emails I'd received since nodding off the night prior. Mostly, I was just following along. Half the emails I received that morning had been incoming. The other half, Holly's responses. And easy to miss among the equipment bids, installation timelines, and countless inspections was a thread with a simple subject line: "Two Addresses." It sounded innocent enough. But it was the beginning of a perilous journey of which my dear friend and business partner, Holly Fox, would nearly lose her mind. Consider this a testament to a great hummingbird chase of historically preposterous proportions. Myself, only a witness. And now, narrator.

Like me, Holly awoke that day and consumed a morning cup of coffee. But while I played the role of spectator, Holly entered a caffeine-induced burst of aggressive productivity—following up, providing signatures, and politely, and sometimes less politely, prodding contractors, inspectors, and city officials to deliver whatever it was that she had been promised. And while the two of us caught up over the phone, discussing the many checks for us to check that day, our focus turned to this annoying issue with Found Oyster's address.

Holly called me. "Adam, you're not going to believe this. Well, I guess *you* will believe it." I could hear the furious tapping of a secondary conversation Holly was having through her keyboard. "I just got off the phone with this guy at the $#*&% department. They're saying *all* of our plans have been issued under the *wrong* address. And that we need to stop work immediately."

"I don't understand."

"Well, apparently '4880 Fountain Ave' has been operating under a 'commonly known as' address, and they're saying we need to *completely resubmit* under a different, apparently *correct*, address."

Holly had been tangled in a web of permitting since we'd first signed the lease. All the time we'd been working on the menu or hosting pop-ups or designing the space, she had been navigating the complex layers of approvals for everything from our liquor license to neighborhood guidelines for signage. Like I said, this is just one story, one of many.

"That's not good," I replied.

"No. It is not good."

"Well! Just another day in the restaurant business. We'll figure it out, Holly Fox."

"You can be quite an obnoxious optimist at times."

"Not an optimist, Holly. I simply expect the occasional ass kicking to be an unavoidable part of life."

Over the next few months, Holly would spend a significant amount of her time investigating what our second, *secret*, "true" address really was. But the various departments overseeing the development of Found Oyster couldn't quite agree on which address was "correct." The 4880 address was *incorrect*, some said. Found Oyster was located at *4878* Fountain Ave. *No, no, no!* other departments proclaimed. No plans could be approved, stamped, and issued for 4878 Fountain Ave. The address *is* 4880 Fountain Ave. And while the antidote for multiple-address disorder remained opaque, the consequences of our condition were moon-jelly clear. We were at a dead stop. And at deadly risk.

And so Holly began to appear at the various city departments tangled in our double-address misadventure. At 7:30 AM, as the city's bureaucratic offices sprung to life, she would materialize. Sometimes distraught. Sometimes demanding. Sometimes desperate. And sometimes threatening damnation. All part of a strategic plan to build sympathy, dread, compassion, and, ultimately, the understanding that she would simply not go away. And it was not until an inspector from the $#*&% department, exploding with righteousness, demanded that Holly never again mention 4880 *or* 4878, *nor* again appear in his office, *nor* speak of this moment to anyone, that our cage was unlocked. With a single stroke of a pen, Found Oyster became 4878 Fountain Ave.

But alas, the bureaucratic barons from above had not had their fill of poor Holly Fox. And the problem that had appeared resolved opened a new chapter of obnoxious obstruction. USPS stopped delivering the mail. For them, 4880 Fountain Ave *was* the correct address. Our neighbor, Sam of the bodega, was located at 4878. The confusion created collapse. And suddenly neither Found, nor Sam, was receiving mail.

To find resolution, we hired an "expeditor," essentially a city planning version of "the Wolf." Our available budget ticking further and further downward. The final result: Found Oyster would operate under its *commonly known as* address. Back where we started. At 4880 Fountain Ave. At least we were once again receiving all the bills we needed to pay.

The DMV Over and Over. And Over. And Over. And How to Get Through It.

Navigating the permitting process for a restaurant is like visiting the DMV on repeat. Your path will include quite a bit of office work and office workers, and it may feel, especially for naturally fidgety restaurant people, like things are moving at the speed of a walnut. But maintaining an empathetic approach is what will pilot your project across the chilly seas of indifference. Even when confronted with contempt by overworked overseers, it's important to stay positive. Even when treated like a contemptuous kindergartener, remain polite. Or at least do the best you can. Smile through your teeth and keep moving forward. One bedraggled swamp foot at a time. And do whatever you can to appear as a human being—and not a case number.

Hammers and Nails

Finally, we enter the grand circus of construction. Three rings of plumbers, electricians, mill workers, metalworkers, low-voltage installers, painters, and equipment vendors all juggled to the beat of our budget while prancing along a seventy-foot-high trapeze with no safety net. Despite the massive effort required to reach this point, it was only now that we pushed our full stack of chips onto the table. Our financial resources were depleting at a faster rate than in any previous stage of development. To stay on track we would need to coordinate a million little things and keep them from crashing into each other, with even the tiniest of errors carrying the potential to create a sphere-of-death disaster. But it was moments like these in which Holly was most truly in her element.

The process of building Found Oyster would now require a raging torrent of decision-making. And although Jake would be leading the process, that did not mean Holly would simply sit back and watch him work. To maintain momentum, she would remain on call for the endless series of questions that would surely arise. And this river of concern would not cease until the space was formally delivered as an operational restaurant. Holly never took a day off. She cared for Found Oyster like a mother bird, purging herself into the trembling mouth of an ever-needy restaurant beak. Prodding and pushing and pulling the restaurant towards maturation.

And to provide constructive answers to the ongoing flow of construction questions, Holly had to overcome the natural fear of sounding like a moron. Often, the questions she asked were ones that our Carhartt-wearing peers found elementary. But if it was going to cost more to plumb the bar in a certain way, Holly may have requested a brief class on why water moves through pipes in a certain way. And dare a grizzled tradesman treat an honest inquiry with disdain. I recall a particularly ill-mannered electrician speaking down to Holly from a pedestal of electrical superiority: "Listen, *lady*. Things just need to be done a certain way. I don't need to tell you how I do my work. I'm an electrician. You're not."

Holly responded like she'd just finished the final sip of a mint julep. "I'm so sorry, *guy*. But given that you *supposedly* studied to be an electrician, you may have noticed that you're laying conduit on the wrong wall."

Part of what made Holly such an incredible restaurant builder was her willingness to dig into even the tiniest minutia within minutiae and make sure that minutia was done correctly. I tend to approach projects with a rubber mallet; Holly carries a scalpel. And as the skeleton of Found Oyster began to be cut into the literal concrete and steel of whatever address you want to believe on Fountain Ave, redoing work would now mean power tools instead of painter's tape.

So began a quick succession of trades installing the rough portion of the project—"trades" being plumbers, electricians, carpenters, and other boot-wearing specialists, and "rough" meaning any work that needed completion before the walls went up and the floor went down. And once their work had been completed, it was time for our first round of physical inspections. A seemingly mundane stretch of our journey, it was anything but. Each and every inspection had the potential to produce ulcer-inducing delays. For, despite having assembled a complete team of architects and contractors and expeditors, inspections covering such a broad range of tiny details, and conducted by human beings, guarantees inconsistencies. And what was approved in a brightly lit office may or may not be approved by that same department's clipboard-carrying inspector on the ground. Thus, the worrying.

And worrying, as it turned out, was an appropriate emotion. Inspectors found that our sewer line was too steep. *Or was it too gradual?* The ceiling above the bar was not a "clean, washable surface." *Even though it was out of reach of the world's tallest man on a stool.* An inspector measured every inch of shelving to ensure we had the "required amount of dry storage." *But what if we just needed more refrigeration?* Found Oyster would get tossed around, from department to department, like a salmon at Pike Place.

But alas, it's best not to dwell on spilt life savings. And we eventually received all of our necessary permits. Framing now turned into furniture. And the materials that Holly had meticulously sourced began to arrive. Slats of polished wood were installed beneath a solid-oak bar top. We felt our elbows dig into the grain for the first time. The carpenter completed our library-like, backbar shelving. Ceiling fans brought movement to the space. And with "cool" lighting being the pea under Holly's mattress, every light fixture, dimmer, and bulb had been hand selected to create a warm, complexion-improving glow.

Holly hired her sister, Alyssa, a talented fine artist and willing to offer family pricing, to assist in designing the restaurant, paint unique art for the space, and create the branding, logo, and menu design. And now, etched into the front window, just above our lone surviving booth, we had the name of the restaurant emblazoned in gold. Well, no, I guess we didn't have the budget for gold, but it said "Found Oyster" in the window. And we were feeling good.

Found Oyster was starting to look like Found Oyster. And Found Oyster was starting to *feel* like Found Oyster. But looking and feeling like a restaurant and operating as a restaurant are two very different things. Soon, we would be handed the keys—not to a construction site but to a restaurant. And with those keys, a thunderous avalanche of work. With a completion timeline that had always been described by us as "unknown," Holly, Joe, Ari, and I, at very long last, started to consider when might be the first day of service. But with a final round of inspections lying before us like the front door of the McCallister family home, we prepared ourselves for one last set of traps.

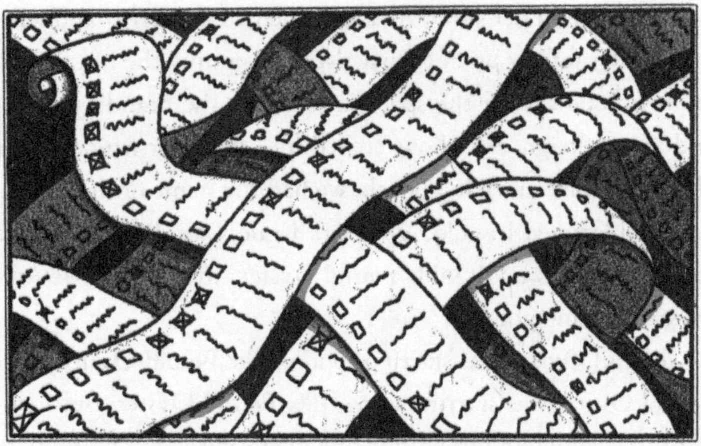

Synchronizing the Greatest Show on Earth

If a prospectus serves as an investment lighthouse, a "critical path," or CP, will be your project-management GPS. A CP is the ultimate checklist, from architecture to zoning. It will give you exact coordinates of where you stand and where you're heading. And while every project may require a slightly different list of concerns, all projects require a list. And I think you'll find that the simple act of personally preparing this planning scorecard will act as a stress reliever of sorts. The CP acts as a weighted blanket to drape on your lap and reclaim the nice, fuzzy feeling of control. Whenever you feel overwhelmed, turn to your list, and pat your own back, and tell yourself that everything is going to be OK. It's all going to be OK. Start with one check, then the next check, and keep checking checks until there are no more checks to check. *It's all going to be OK.*

• 10 •

Restaurant People

I had always assumed that I'd eventually move on from restaurants. When I first started waiting tables, my only intention was to make money for various high school vices and maybe play a few rounds of the regional, *northeastern* Massachusetts card game known as 45s. Serving food from plastic bags, reciting plastic-sounding "selling lines" learned from a Human Resources video in the liquor closet, and squeezing plastic lids onto infernal plastic kids' cups was not necessarily inspiring. But my career continued, almost incidentally, when I attended college at UMass Amherst, locally nicknamed "the Zoo." Unable to pick a major that sounded appealing, I chose something that sounded familiar, "Hotel, Restaurant, and Tourism Administration," or HRTA, also known as HRT-*easy*-A.

And if HRTA had a middling reputation as the black sheep of UMass's business program, which it was, then the restaurant division was the redheaded, one-legged, glue-sniffing stepchild. In the five years I spent in the program, and no, I did *not* graduate with a master's degree, it often felt like faculty were attempting to talk us out of our chosen profession. Hotels were *good.* Restaurants, *bad.* It probably didn't help that Marriott was the leading financial contributor to the program. I recall a guest speaker, some suited fella who had wheedled his way through some corporate maze and up to the podium of a UMass auditorium, who chose to spend much of his time ranting about the long hours and shit money of the restaurant business. Hotels offered better pay, more time off, travel benefits, and a life. At first, I listened.

I took a job at a fine hotel in Boston directly after college. A big fancy spot constructed from the granite upon which America was built. But I didn't last long. Feeling choked out by the daily tying of a tie and drowning in boredom by the water bubbler, I missed restaurants. Mostly, I missed restaurant *people.* I realized that there is no workplace on Earth where a more diverse group—ethnically, culturally, economically, politically, and whatever else the world likes to divide itself by—shares such a similar experience. Maybe not in harmony, per se. But better yet, in a kitchen-sink mélange. And in that moment, I realized that it was the *people I worked with* that would determine if I liked my career. Or if I hated it. The job, itself, was secondary.

And I soon learned that restaurants *did* provide much of what were proclaimed as benefits limited to hotel work. As a server, I was able to move from Western Massachusetts to Martha's Vineyard. Spending my days at the beach and nights waiting tables. Then I moved back to Boston. Then I moved to San Diego. Then to LA. I worked in restaurants at every stop. I started seeking out ways to move up. First as a lead server. Then a floor manager. And then, as a general manager. Falling on my ass but learning all the time. Growing my confidence. Making a living. And I learned what it took to lead a group of humans through the choppy waters of restaurant life.

It started by admitting that human beings are, indeed, *human.* And despite their position on something like a restaurant team, each person's own life protrudes far beyond that of their workplace. People have kids. Spouses. In-laws. Exes. They owe rent. They have to buy groceries. And they get flat tires. Sometimes they lose people they care about. And sometimes they meet new people they care about. And sometimes they get too drunk. And sometimes they challenge you. And each and every one of them, each and every one of *us*, is incapable of being anything other than a human being. But the work needs to get done. And everyone needs to do their part. Standards must be upheld—even on a tough day, even when it's raining, even when you have a hangover.

Despite what you may have heard, the customer is most certainly not always right. Nor is the staff. Nor am I. But in this most endless of endurance races, and with so much dependence on human beings working and patronizing the restaurant, what mattered most was doing the respectable thing. The reasonable thing. One could even say the right thing. And by focusing my time and energy on building culture based on mutual, unceasing, and nonnegotiable respect, an environment was formed in which trust could exist. And if respect could, and should, be demanded for all and from all, then trust most certainly could not. It has to be earned.

Handle the Mess

To build a strong culture, it's important that you clean the vomit, literally and metaphorically. The easiest way to hold a crew accountable is to personally tackle the least desirable tasks in the restaurant. Not the mundane daily tasks that are unavoidable in the restaurant industry. For yes, someone must peel shallots all day long. It means stepping into *emergencies* without hesitation. Handling a disgruntled guest. Kicking out an obnoxious drunk. Cleaning up said drunk's puke in the bathroom. Counting inventory on New Year's morning. Locking the doors for a closing server whose section got rocked. Leadership is about stepping up in the moments when *everything* goes wrong. And it is in these moments that trust is established. *Trust,* being the thing that makes managing restaurants financially, and mentally, viable.

> To do this job and have a life, you need to know that people have your back. So, start out by having theirs.

Building a Team

There is a single moment when a construction site becomes a restaurant, its passage confirmed by *smell.* Aromas of dust and paint and glue are replaced by *something cooking.* It doesn't matter what; it could be butter melting or bread toasting or garlic sweating or chicken roasting. It's a moment worth celebrating. A moment worth commemorating. A moment to reflect on all the obstacles overcome, challenges met, and victories won. This is a wonderful moment. And like many wonderful moments in the restaurant business, a fleeting one. When the smell of bacon rendering for clam chowder filled the room at whatever address it was we occupied on Fountain Ave, we had our own restaurant. And with it, a lot to do.

Found Oyster was now, more or less, alive. And as any parent will tell you, creating a living thing is quite a bit of fun. And any knucklehead, regardless of their capacity to do so, can participate in the process. But *raising* a living thing is hard. And it's a long road. The very *being* of Found Oyster would now be comprised of people. In many cases, people we did not yet know. And we would need to transform a group of strangers into a band of oyster-shucking, guest-serving, self-bussing, door-hosting, peerless professionals—*with style*—a unique skill set unlikely encountered on the street. Found Oyster would be a culture unique to itself. And all that we'd hoped for, dreamed of, and invested in would now be put to the test. To realize the full potential of Found Oyster, we needed a crew.

Hiring is the single greatest responsibility of a restaurant operator. Well, hiring, and not spreading salmonella. You see, every person on the team would represent a ripple in the human ecosystem that would be Found Oyster. And in the physical closeness of restaurant work, each employee provides their own seasoning to the stockpot of team morale. And in the extreme closeness of Found Oyster, each person would be contributing to a single serving of personality soup. So, like making any tasty potage, we set out to find the right balance between the ingredients.

Per always, we tried to fill the team with people we had collectively worked with in the past. Only reaching beyond our network after exhausting all leads within it. There was much to consider. Career experience. Work ethic. Personal goals. Personal life. Personality. Energy. Aura. Trustworthiness. Hygiene. And so on. Our top priority was identifying compatibility. Well, compatibility and NBA-grade shucking skills. Our interview process was not scientific, for people are not formulas and interviews are not restaurant work. You see, it's hard to determine "fit" without trying something on for size. And nothing would have revealed a potential hire's suitability like seeing them mixed into the frenetic energy of restaurant service. A working interview, known as a "stage," pronounced "*stahzh,*" in the restaurant world, is a better interview. But as a yet-to-be-operating establishment, there would be no opportunity to see how potential staff responded to the action. We'd have to go with our gut.

And although I could write volumes about the wonderful people that worked at Found Oyster during those early days, I shall focus on a few who forever shaped how the restaurant would be run.

Cue the montage.

The Shucking Star

Meredith Brugler would act as the guinea pig that proved, or disproved, Found Oyster's entire premise. A native Ohioan, she would be the restaurant's first shucking bartender. Meredith joined us from Leon's in Charleston. Yes, *that* Leon's. The same restaurant that Ari had opened as executive chef. And like discovering an oyster-culling cheat code, Meredith would soon display that the lines between front of house and back of house need not only be blurred—they could be erased. The first seafood-slaying rock star in LA, Meredith became a symbol, I think, of what a dynamic restaurant person is truly capable of.

As you imagine how your restaurant will function, remember it will be people who prove or disprove your theories. *Never accept what is written of restaurants as gospel.* Even the most sacred doctrines of this business, aside from the cleanliness bits, can be cast aside. Rules can be rewritten for your own reasons. Systems redesigned for new intents and purposes. And when it comes to people, people like Meredith, versatility is worth seeking. Seeking and *headlining.* And with Meredith's help, the old French brigade, as it had been taught to me, at least, was at long last dead.

The Trusted Hand

A Scot by way of Texas, Rory Cameron arrived at Found Oyster with an established skill set gleaned from his time working alongside Ari at Hayden. And it was this preexisting set of skills that provided Rory with the capacity to assume one of the most challenging roles in the restaurant. You see, Rory's station, from which much of the restaurant's food would flow, came with a slight complication. Or maybe not so slight. Like the shuckers, Rory was asked to serve his end of the bar. But unlike an oyster, which, if paused mid-shuck, will remain in its suspended state, the food Rory was pulling off a plancha could not be paused mid-cook—it'd burn. But despite the constant pressure, even in the most frantic moments of service, Rory could be found slowly swaying, middle-school-style, while toasting hot dog buns and mixing lobster salad and charming guests with his old-world brogue.

It's hard to overstate the importance of calm in a restaurant. Especially a new one. Framing your staff around people, unflappable under pressure, builds the kind of foundation that can withstand the inevitable storms of restaurant work. And those storms never seemed to bother Rory much. You, too, will need people to dance through challenges. And as you watch them sway, I think you'll find that a little calm, charm, and a touch of rhythm will solve much of what troubles you. For sometimes, all you can do is dance, smile, and work your way through disaster.

The Hired Gun

Peter Westberg represented an older, wiser, gentler generation at Found. A writer by trade, Peter could be counted on to set a good example, to make people laugh, and to cover the shifts of his younger, more hungover compatriots. And it was not uncommon to hear the understated brilliance of hospitality he'd learned from that older, wiser, gentler restaurant group in New York. You know, the one with all the accolades and strong corporate culture and their own books. Peter's business card, offered with the upmost subtlety, and with a supernatural ability to recognize the perfect moment, read only: *Peter Westberg. Professional Server.*

In a business based on creating joy, the ability to draw smiles from your crew will be what draws smiles from your guests. Peter, and veterans like him, have the ability to navigate much of what a restaurant will experience for the first time—*not for the first time.* Often, with humor. For seasoned pros like Peter, even the most novel of restaurant experiences is like retelling an old story. All they have to do is cycle through old punch lines, disarming all, and endearing themselves, and the restaurant, to all who cross their paths.

The Best of Sweetgreen

As his nickname indicates, Mike Davis joined Found Oyster directly from the culinary capital of Kale. And if he hadn't arrived to his interview on a skateboard, one would have been forgiven for assuming so. But despite his years in the back of house, Mike had never, at that time, shucked an oyster. At least not professionally.

That changed quickly. Dedicated to his own daily improvement, Mike became the most noticeably changed person on the team. A seed from corporate kitchens, Mike emerged as a sea sponge of every imaginable skill. Running every station. Butchering every variety of fish. Serving every guest in his vicinity. And if one had any doubt of his dedication, they need only follow him along his sixty-traffic-light commute, on a bicycle, to understand the extent of his commitment. And it was commitment, commitment and *time*, that transformed Mike from shy salad maker to the first chef de cuisine of Found Oyster. An example of getting the best out of people by giving them room to get the best out of themselves. Patience, and a path, are really all it takes.

An Ace Up Our Sleeve

Mike Santos and I first met while waiting tables on Martha's Vineyard. Already working with Last Word on our consulting projects, we'd brought him into Found Oyster with the expectation that he be, well, *himself.* A Portuguese immigrant, Mike was the first person in his family to speak English and had been the family's designated translator (and negotiator) since age eight. And Joe could rely on Mike to assist with problems with staffing, programming the POS, finding vendor contacts, hood cleanings, or any other frustration. If Joe was a server short, or a shucker short, or was near short-circuiting, he could turn to Mike.

You, too, will need someone to do the dirty work. Someone to find those unfortunate crumbs of important but odious work that so often get stuck in the cracks. You will need someone who can organize payroll. Program a POS in five minutes. Negotiate insurance. Negotiate cleaning contracts. Negotiate all that needs negotiating, really. You need someone who can show up and fill *any* role with just a few minutes' training. As you assemble your own restaurant team, remember: There is simply no such thing as too many great people in a restaurant opening.

IIIIIIII

Much of what each of these montage-worthy folks brought to the restaurant *stayed* at the restaurant long after they left. Their presence—still felt at Found Oyster to this very day.

The World's Most Concise Job Description

Be on time. Treat others with respect. Focus.
Be honest. Dress for the job. Smell good. And keep it professional.
Learn the material.

> Practice. Practice. Practice.
>
> Keep improving. Keep growing.
>
> Take a deep breath. Failure is OK. But it's not to be repeated.
>
> We do things like this. Step by step. Always the same.
>
> Cook the fish like this. Shuck an oyster like that. Pour wine like a pro.
>
> Bussing is an art. Study the masters.
>
> Write stuff down. Don't drop stuff. Taste and smell everything.
>
> Make them laugh. Listen to them cry. Learn their names.
>
> Always the same. But make it yours.
>
> Every job matters.
>
> Keep improving. Keep growing.
>
> Dig in for the long haul.
>
> We need each other to make it work. So, let's make it work.

Get the Reps

With the team assembled, Found Oyster began its own version of restaurant rehearsals. Training meant getting the crew on their feet, bumping into one another, working through the kinks until everyone was dancing to the same tune. Well, working through as many kinks as our quickly depleting budget would allow. The closer we got to the opening, the more we straddled the line between the fatal risk of overspending and the equally fatal risk of underperforming.

The first moments of training at Found Oyster occurred like most "first moments"—with clenched smiles and brief conversations with no destination and nobody knowing where to put their hands. Seeing this, I, with great pride, fulfilled one of my most sacred duties at Found Oyster. I kicked off training with a motivating, heartfelt, and self-deprecating speech in an attempt to pump up the crew while disarming that most counterproductive of emotions—*embarrassment*. I did my best to clear the air of discomfort and free the group from the fear of looking like dumbasses. To prepare for our first guests, we would need to be comfortable falling on our faces before they showed up.

When I'd finished speaking, Peter appeared magically beside me, and in the most courteous manner, he whispered, "Hey, boss, I gotta say . . . I've never seen anybody get up there and actually *encourage* people to screw up. Really excited to see how this plays out."

"That's not how they did things in *New York*, Peter?"

"*No, no, no*. Yeah, no. They didn't."

"Well, I meant we should screw up *now* rather than *later*. But I guess we're going to find out."

"We sure are, boss. Hey, did I ever tell you about what Danny Meyer used to say about training?"

"You haven't."

"It was pretty great. But you don't want to hear about that right now. You do you."

Training for a restaurant opening is like training for a mountaineering expedition. And like mountaineering, it's vital to start with the fundamentals. For the assumption of preexisting abilities in restaurants, like on mountains, can lead to a very long fall. So, it was with a principled expectation of total ignorance that we began training with the foundational basics of restaurant service. And yes, this meant that Mike and Peter would be practicing table bussing. And yes, this meant that Rory and Meredith would be practicing how to cut fish. Everyone would be practicing things they already knew how to do. The reason for this was simple: We needed everyone doing these things *the same way*. The Found Oyster way.

We fired oversized tickets and shucked excess oysters and cooked for ghosts. Overbooked an imaginary waitlist and tried to find our way out of it. We prepared, carried, delivered, and explained dramatically overvaried raw bar towers. We ran tray races, filling cocktail trays with overflowing glassware and laying completely unrealistic obstacles between the bar and a phantom table. We ran "mock service," attempting to create something that felt, at least a little bit, like real service. And despite the expense, we used all real products. For one can learn to shuck oysters by shelling peanuts no better than one can learn the aromas of wine by sniffing Pepsi.

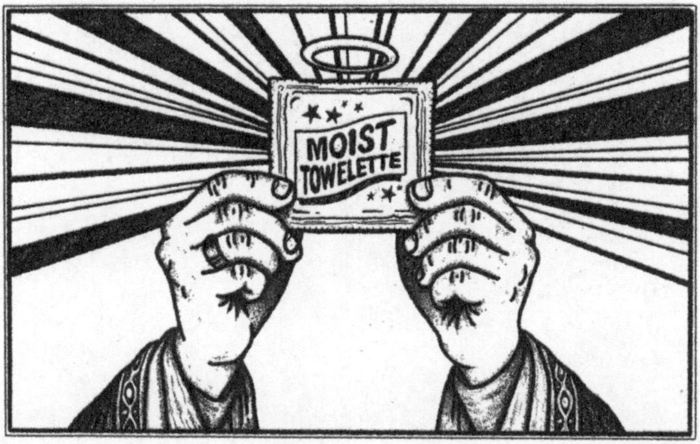

Service and Hospitality

Many a Tony-restaurant-Robbins have sufficiently preached the values of hospitality and its differentiation from service. So, I shall be brief. Service is a series of steps—an operating procedure, really. A procedure followed by everyone to ensure the *same* quality of product is delivered to each guest. Service acts as the guidelines for consistency. Hospitality, on the other hand, requires individuality. It is the process of creatively delivering empathy. Each diner wants to be treated differently. Some formally. Some not. Some at arm's length. Some, desiring a pal at their table. But everyone—and I mean everyone—will want a clean plate and some wet ones after a pile of peel-and-eat shrimps. Service. And hospitality. They both matter. Train accordingly.

• 11 •

Stepping from the Ledge

Uh-oh . . . Who's getting fired?" Joe walked into the restaurant to find Holly, Ari, and me sitting at the bar, leaning just a little too low.

Holly sighed. "That's a good question, Joe. Maybe all of us." Joe grabbed a stool and waited for Holly to continue. "The $#*&% department is suddenly demanding *two* bathrooms to operate with beer and wine. Why they have a policy about *bathroom counts for beverage service, when they're not even responsible for the sale of alcohol*, is beyond me. There's a 'variance' process, but it's not guaranteed to be approved."

The four of us sat on freshly unpacked black stools and rested our elbows on the freshly polished wooden bar and shuffled our feet on freshly laid tile. The shelves were lined with wine bottles and boxes of oyster crackers and statues and statuettes and *tasteful* seaside decor of all kinds. Stacks of folded napkins lay next to stacks of plates, next to stacks of silverware. All tightly organized like a general store.

Ari was cradling one of his temples. "Alright, so how do we get this 'variance'?"

"Well, the approval process requires an on-site inspection," Holly explained, "but—and here is the kicker—they'll only inspect and approve an *operating* restaurant. They won't come unless we're serving guests."

"You've got to be fucking kidding me. Why?" Ari was now cradling both his temples with two hands.

Holly was about to respond when I interjected: "Well . . . Like Clint Eastwood said, *Reason's got nothing to do with it.* They say 'jump,' we jump. Or . . . I think that's what he said."

Joe giggled. Ari snickered. And Holly held the bridge of her nose.

After eighteen months of planning, permitting, building, and worrying, we believed we were close. One by one, and not without a bit of jostling, we'd passed our inspections. But at the very last minute, this flaming fastball of foolishness had been thrown at our heads. The $*$&# department was not responsible for overseeing the sale of alcohol. That entity had already approved us. But some piece of #&!* at the $#*&% department discovered a secret $*#*$^% decree that required two bathrooms to sell beer and wine, regardless of the restaurant's size or seat count. And only now, with a fully built Found Oyster, were they letting us know.

Joe asked about the elephant in the room. "What happens if they don't grant us the variance?"

The three of us turned to Holly. "It would not be good. In fact, it would be very bad," she said. "We would be forced to choose between operating without beer and wine or building a second bathroom. Leaving us with maybe fifteen seats."

"Fifteen seats and two bathrooms," I thought out loud.

Sometimes it felt as if a cartoon rain cloud was following us around. Dark and stormy and shooting bolts of lightning crashing directly into Found Oyster. We had successfully transformed an empty space on Fountain Ave into a restaurant that closely resembled the one we'd dreamed of, but "turning it on" meant expending our remaining funds on product and people. What would happen if we were not granted the variance? Could Found Oyster survive serving iced tea and soda instead of beer and wine? We were quite certain it would not.

"We can't open Found Oyster without beer and wine," I whispered.

"Well, we're going to have to," Holly responded.

"Maybe we don't. We need to be operating to receive this inspection, but we don't need to be operating as Found Oyster."

"Go on, Adam." Holly braced her ear into her shoulder.

"I mean, we *can't* open Found Oyster without beer and wine. The mere thought of it makes me want to puke down my shirt. So, we create a *new* restaurant. Something temporary. Something that shows we're still not *fully* Found Oyster, yet. Another pop-up."

"That's interesting," Holly commented.

"We call it something simple. Like, the 'Clam Shack.'" I was on my feet now. "And we limit hours to a few days a week. Lunch only. And *when* we get our variance, we fully launch Found Oyster."

"The Clam Shack!" Joe, too, was back on his feet. "I love it!"

"The Clam Shack . . ." Holly had gears spinning in her pupils. "OK, I like it, too."

Ari looked revived. "Fuck it, I'm in."

Joe was bouncing as he said, "Let's get some tees printed! I'm thinking we do oysters, clams, lobster rolls, tostadas, and chowdaaaaa!" He was smiling like a cat.

We ran the Clam Shack for about a month. Three days a week. Four hours a day. Just enough to satisfy our operating requirement. We offered an abbreviated menu. Raw oysters. Fried oysters. Wedge salad. Lobster roll. Tostadas. Coleslaw. Lipton iced tea. Coca-Cola. Sprite. And chowdaaaaa. A signature tagline for our checks, written by Joe, properly explained the experience, *Wham bam thank you clam.* And we served just enough people to not lose money. But while the Clam Shack had blossomed into a low-pressure party that we truly enjoyed, no one slept the night before the *#^$ inspector finally arrived to issue a decision on our variance. Bleary eyed and walking on broken seashells, we awaited our fate.

"Ah, this place is great! What a tiny little spot." Roger, as his name tag indicated, was draped in khaki, carrying a clipboard, and apparently not too concerned about our single restroom. "I'm guessing the bathroom is back through this hallway? Yep. OK, great. And the kitchen stops, where? Oh! It really is a tiny spot." Two minutes after entering Found Oyster, Roger was done. "Well, guys, there's obviously no space for a second restroom. Certainly not just to add some tasty alcoholic beverages to the joint! How many seats you got in here, anyway?"

"There are twenty-six seats," Holly answered through a bear-trap smile.

"Twenty-six seats?! Can you make any money with twenty-six seats?"

Holly's smile sliced deeper into her cheeks. "Well, *Roger*, we're certainly going to try!"

"OK, then. Well, uh. I'm going to . . . Uh, I'm going to get back to the office on Monday and will submit the papers! My boss needs to sign off, and you guys will be all set."

"And how long might that be?" Holly asked.

"He's usually pretty quick, I guess. Everything should be good to go by the end of next week."

"OK. Thank you so much, Roger. Is there a number I can reach you at? Just to follow up?"

"Yes, ma'am. Here's my card."

Holly accepted the card, and Roger ran for the door.

A Marathon That Ends at the Starting Line

Building a restaurant is a bit like completing a marathon only to find yourself back at the starting line. With every sink plumbed. Permit signed off on. Wall painted. License acquired. Art hung. Staff trained. Recipe finalized. And money spent. After all the hard work, investment, and risk, this is the moment that risk multiplies. *This is the moment that may make or break your restaurant.* And beyond the obvious challenge of winning over your customers that lies ahead, less evident challenges, no less important, hide on the fringes. The challenge I'm referring to: the establishment of the many professional relationships that will define how you run your business. I speak, of course, of your *vendors.* Each vendor representing an opportunity for your restaurant to be better or worse off. Each vendor relationship as important as those that I've already described.

And as many wonderful vendors in the world that exist to serve restaurants, and there *are* many passionate, honest, and transparent wholesalers in the world, there are others who expect your fatigue from what came before and what still lies ahead to mean a lapse in judgment. A lapse they can take advantage of. A lapse that can cost you your business. Each vendor relationship is a partnership of sorts. Each business supporting the other. Or that's how it's supposed to be. Each partnership, like all partnerships, needs to be vetted before it can be trusted. You will need to regard each new contract with a fresh eye. You will need the energy to negotiate pricing, fees, terms, and delivery schedules. As a restaurant transitions from development to operations, you've got to shake off your fatigue and prepare for a whole new race. It begins sooner than you might think . . .

Final Preparations

We felt mostly operationally prepared and fully financially pressured to open for business. But we needed one *true* practice before we started accepting hard-earned cash. Found Oyster would greet its first guests through a "Friends & Family" service. A dinner service dry run. A service where only those trusted to not talk shit *publicly* are invited. For only when pushed to the brink would we fully grasp how well we had prepared Found Oyster to set sail. And there were sure to be a few leaks.

Now, if you've ever read a cookbook or a Ruth Reichl novel, you're probably familiar with the concept of *mise en place*, translated literally as, "Where shit lives," or something like that. And while I was more than happy to eviscerate the brigade system, there really is no replacement for having stuff in the right place. So based on the team's discoveries during mock services, they set Found Oyster like an experimental chessboard. Found's *mise* now stood like game pieces, polished and perfectly aligned. Water and wine bottles were filled and chilled and aptly organized. Oysters were artistically arranged on shimmering piles of ice. Knives and wine keys and minds were sharpened and appropriately set. Everyone was cleaning what had already been cleaned and organizing what had already been organized.

But just because we were only inviting friends and family didn't mean we weren't nervous. *We were nervous.* This would be our first experience receiving feedback about Found Oyster from a diner's perspective. And only now would we start to hear the truth. What people liked. What they disliked. What they loved. And what they hated. We'd provide comment cards for every guest. Their comments, our *compensation*. With dozens of reviews to consider, and not dreading their public posting, we would have a treasure trove of information to utilize while we made final preparations for accepting the public.

Exactly an hour before guests were due to arrive, we gathered the crew along the bar. Sitting on those black stools were Rory, Meredith, Peter, Sweetgreens, and the rest of our small team. Standing behind the bar, soon to serve as the stage for our shucking stars, were Holly, Joe, Ari, Mike Santos, and little old me. Outside, the sun was going down, but inside, we were amping up. The time had *finally* arrived.

"OK, crew. This is it. The first service of Found Oyster." I rode my adrenaline like a Windsurfer. "First, I want to say thank you. This job is never easy and I'm so grateful to have each of you with us. So, thank you." I paused to mark the moment. "Now! If there is anything I've learned over the years, it's that 'first nights' typically don't go so well. But we're going to change that. Tonight, we are going to blow people's fucking minds. And we're going to do it by *looking like we've been here before*. That's it. If there's a single comment we want to hear tonight, it's 'I can't believe it's your first night! Like, wow!'" Again, I took a brief pause, smiling my big dumb smile, and then continued, "Thank you guys for being here. This job ain't easy, and we know it. So, thank you. It means a lot. Really. Thank you."

There was gentle but heartfelt applause, and I suppressed a stream of joyful tears.

Ari stepped forward and rested his elbows on the service end of the bar. He began, "Alright, y'all . . . You only get to be a part of something like this so often . . . So, let's make the most of it. What's most important tonight is that we stay calm. Even if tickets pile up, which, in all likelihood, *they will*, we're going to maintain our composure and work together. Wait times are not our concern tonight. But we need the product to be *great*. Take your time and do things right. I'll be on point, shuckin' all night. Come to me with anything ya need. And remember, *we're in this together*. Thank you, guys. I'm honored to be here with all of y'all."

The crew applauded once again and, once again, I sucked tears back into my head.

Now it was Holly's turn. Never comfortable as a public speaker, I knew it was *this moment* that she dreaded most. But these moments are important. And Holly, fanning herself with one hand as she spoke, did so, from the heart: "This is such a special moment. I can't tell you guys how good it feels to see *people* in this darling little space. From the moment we signed this lease, almost eighteen months ago if you can believe it, we dreamed of what it would be like to see the restaurant come to *life*. And that didn't happen until all of you arrived. This restaurant is the result of a very, very long road. And I couldn't be prouder to have this group of people as the ones to help us introduce Found Oyster to LA."

There was a clatter of fists along the bar. Gentle clapping had progressed into subtle hoots and less subtle hollers, and I pretended to have something stuck in my eye.

"Wow. I can't believe we're really here, guys." Joe was nearly levitating as he spoke. "This is no longer the Clam Shack. Today is Found Oyster's birthday!" Our small clan of overexcited restaurant hooligans started clapping and banging their fists on the bar. Joe waited like a pastor for the din to settle. "Now, remember, we know *everybody* who's dining with us tonight. But that's not to say we should take this service lightly. This is our last chance to figure shit out before we start getting Yelped."

"*Boooooo*," I hummed. Tears now streaming down my face.

Joe continued, "Most importantly! Let's have fun out there. Keep your heads on a swivel and let's shuck!" It was all hoots and hollers now. We were ready.

And with that, I littered the restaurant with stacks of Post-it notes. The intention being: If you see something, say something. And if too busy, write it down and slap that sucker right on the problem. Bouncing like a beagle while we opened the patinated front door, Holly and I caught each other's eyes. We nodded in mutual excitement. We'd made it. Found Oyster, at long last, was going to meet the world.

What Song Should We Play First?

For most of my adult life, I'd dreamed of owning a restaurant. And in these dreams, a song is always playing. Scorsese-like in its suitability and timing. The scene in the movie when the sounds of the outside world stop. Time slows down. A door is opened. And the hero, or the villain, makes their entry across a red carpet of *sound*. Would it be the Rolling Stones? James Brown? Kendrick? Steely Dan? The theme song from *The A-Team*? After more than a decade of fantasy, it was now time to choose the first song.

But it was Joe, whose passion for movie soundtracks surpassed even my own, who chose the first song. And it *was* the Rolling Stones. And not just one song. Joe played the entire *Exile on Main Street* album. From start to finish. And I had the very great pleasure of watching a group, so recently strangers, harmonize into a strutting, oyster-slaying, wine-spraying restaurant rock and roll band. And although there had been no rock concert lines forming when we first opened Found Oyster, a frenetic energy began to grow in our little restaurant. We weren't packed. But people were happy. *It made me so happy that they were happy.* They ate and drank and smiled and laughed and sometimes cried. All the while, "Tumbling Dice" played in the background. I think Scorsese would've been just as proud as I was.

Holly, Ari, Joe, and I spent most of that first evening adjusting the lights. Obsessively. Us, four partners, in constant discussion about shadows and ambiance and what was too dark and what was too bright. We changed the speed of the ceiling fans over and over again. Trying to create the perfect amount of movement without freezing our guests. We changed the volume of the music every sixty seconds, desperate to find the perfect pitch. And all along the bar, nestled between wine and water glasses, shoved under the rims of plates, covering devoured shellfish towers like piles of dirty snowballs, were crumpled-up paper napkins. I'd become stuck on using stainless-steel napkin dispensers to add an extra element of vintage vibes. But the single-ply, nearly useless paper needed for such vessels had a habit of hiding in any and all cracks. The napkins, and their dispensers, would be gone within a few weeks.

Filter Feeding the Feedback

Don't listen to trolls. Listen to regulars. Don't listen to an old pal who gushes over every dish, drink, and piece of decor. Listen to bartenders. Listen to cooks. Listen to dishwashers. Don't listen to divas. Don't let a positive review go to your head. And don't let a bad one get you down. Consider the source. Consider the timing. Consider compatibility. And whenever given the opportunity, ask questions. Especially in person. Why did you feel that way? What made you say that? How would you do things differently? *Would you order that dish again?* Understanding where information is coming from is the only way to know if it's worth listening to. And remember: It's easy to talk shit. But taking shit calmly, while keeping your head up, well, that shit *is* hard.

• 12 •

Welcome to Found Oyster

There had been no red ribbon cutting or long lines of salivating fans when we opened our little oyster bar. There were, however, *friends*. And soon after, friends of friends. And as we had hoped, we received an early groundswell of support from restaurant folks. Servers and cooks and bartenders and chefs filled the restaurant when we so desperately needed it to be filled. And finally, at long, long last, we were selling food *and* wine. *And* beer. Found Oyster was no longer a dream, or a goal, or a theory. It was a *restaurant*.

A few months into what we hoped would be the long voyage of Found Oyster, we were starting to find our sea legs. A cool breeze of business had started to build. Soon, the restaurant was filling up. All twenty-six seats. Then, we started building a nightly waitlist. There seemed to be a glowing, almost innate, *communal* sensation that something special was happening. People started showing up thirty minutes before we opened to snatch an early seat. They were asking for Ari and Joe and Rory and Peter and Mike and Meredith—by name. And these people who had started as strangers became *regulars*. Who, in turn, became *friends*. And they started to bring *their* friends. Everybody seemed to be talking about Found Oyster. Good things, thank god.

And like a lobster molting its shell, Found Oyster started to grow. And change. Equipment was rearranged. Real wood tables replaced our almost-cardboard originals. Shelving was installed in every nook and cranny until our kitchen appeared as some kind of shimmering steel coral reef. And Ari started expanding the menu. The now-famous bitter lime crab cocktail was created. A beef tartar burger was covered in onion rings. Smoked trout dip was topped with smoked trout roe and served with Ritz crackers. And an ongoing variety of new dishes, often vegetables, started showing up on a chalk-written specials board. Leeks with gribiche. Broccolini with burrata-like whipped tofu. Local peppers grilled and simply dressed in chili threads. The conversation around the restaurant seemed to be getting louder. More good things.

One afternoon, Ari and Joe appeared on the local news, shucking oysters and making scallop tostadas, right after the local weather forecast. Found Oyster started appearing on lists of the best places to eat in Los Angeles. The restaurant was written into a TV pilot. People were proudly claiming to have *discovered* the restaurant. They were calling it *their* place. I even saw somebody rocking a Found Oyster hat while I was back in Boston. What had started as an intermittent breeze was now a steady gale, pushing us into territory we'd never imagined. And as the seasons changed, so did we. Found Oyster was exploding with creativity, patronage, and positivity. It had taken so long for everything to happen so fast. And as 2019 wound down, we *knew* that 2020 was to be the year of Found Oyster.

IIIIIIII

"Joe!" I shouted over the music. "You might need to wear that thing every night."

"Fuck that! It's hot as hell in here."

"Well, buddy, you should have thought about that before you put it on. It's just too good." I stood back to review Joe's full figure. "Yeah, man. I think we need to consider this your official uniform."

"Maybe if you install a little fan in here."

"Fair enough. *Listen*, Joe. You wear the *lobstah* head, you keep your job."

It was New Year's Eve. And Joe's typical features had been replaced by the gigantic, bright-red felt head of a fuzzy crustacean. His outfit completed by a buttery black tuxedo. And this Shaq-sized, James Bondian *Joestacean* had been elegantly pouring a magnum of champagne for guests along the bar. They were smiling and laughing and eating and drinking and flirting and celebrating. They had their elbows resting on the knotty bar, and they played footsie with their dates on the checkered floor as they sipped wine from short little wineglasses that made the wine nerds go berserk. And they slammed oyster after oyster after oyster. And everything was right in the world.

"Need some more champagne, *dood*?" Filling my cup before I could answer, Joe continued, excitedly, "We're cranking, man. And I recognize half the people in here, too. I guess one could even call them our *regulars*! Lots of raw bar. Lots of lobster rolls. Tons of tostadas. And bottle after bottle of bubbles going out."

"Yo! Pour me some of that." Ari never stopped shucking as he made his request from behind the bar.

"Yes, Chef! You guys good back there?"

"Of course, we're good back here. Hey! Fill that glass up. You holdin' out on me?"

"Sorry, Chef."

"Anybody going to invite *me* for a toast?" Holly joined with a three-cheers smile.

"Ayyyy, Happy New Year's, you guys!" I yelled over the din. "I guess this is the time when we're supposed to say something pretty, but . . . all I can think of right now is that we fucking did it. We did it."

Holly raised her glass of wine. "Guys, we fucking did it. To Found Oyster!"

Smiling, Ari, Joe, and I raised our glasses to Holly's. And as if driven by some deep, long-dormant Neanderthal instinct, we began to howl—a unified, guttural, instinctual howl that can only be unearthed by participating in a successful wolf hunt. And we toasted with an unspoken understanding that can only be gained by having been challenged, and by having met those challenges. *Together.* And having stuck together through so much bullshit. Through all the ups and downs and fears and anxieties and feelings of helplessness. We had done it together. And now, there was nothing that could stop us.

"Hey! What time is it?" Ari looked at his phone. "Oh, shit! Guys! It's 8:50. Let's get ready to drop the ball!"

"On it, Chef!" Joe went running off to retrieve another magnum.

Sitting back on my stool, I noticed my barstool neighbor looking back and forth between me and her watch. Obviously puzzled by what she had just overheard, I let her in on a little surprise we'd been holding back: "There is nothing wrong with your watch—"

"So sorry! I didn't mean to intrude. It's just . . . Well, are you the *owner* of this place?"

"I'm fortunate enough to be one of them, yes."

"You look so young! Well, congratulations on all your success. But was I mistaken, or did I just hear you say something about dropping the ball?"

"You most certainly did."

"But it's not even nine PM."

"Well, it's not yet nine PM *here*. But our license requires that we close by eleven." I turned towards the woman, smiled, and raised my glass to hers. "So, we're dropping the ball on Cape Cod time."

And I watched guest after guest be confronted by the giant *Joestacean*. Each being informed of our upcoming toast on Eastern Standard Time with a glass of champagne. And the laughter that resulted, well, it made this salty ol' Masshole tear up . . . again. I sat back and watched as an Irish jig of shucking and serving and new friendships took place before me. And I experienced what was for me a novel sensation. I felt at home. But I was at work. Fully content. But at work. Playing. But at work. With my friends. But working. Found Oyster had become my favorite place in the world. But this was my *job*. One little room. One gigantic ocean of feelings. Guests were loving the restaurant. And they were loving our team. And I was beyond grateful. And joyful. And relieved. Each guest that left with a smile was vindication for all that we had risked and all the work and all the hassles. It made it all worth it.

The Long Journey

As you watch your dream transition into something real, many phases of its life lie before you. This is particularly true for restaurants. From your mother's brother's former roommate to local chefs to the food media, everybody shows up at first. Then, when the newness has worn off, they stop in less often. If at all. And that's when the voyage really begins.

As your own restaurant ship slips from its harbor and into the ocean of time, you'll need to be prepared for anything. To keep a steady keel in rough waters. You can expect business to slow down in a rainstorm. Or halt entirely under hail. You can expect increased sales from an article on supporting local restaurants. Or dropping off a cliff from a trendy new diet. Likes and dislikes change. And a single cultural event may forever alter the way people eat or drink (look at what the movie *Sideways* did to poor ol' Merlot). You'll need to constantly reevaluate the financial puzzle of your restaurant, first predicted way back when, and creatively find ways to piece things together. Finagling your way through inventory reports, staffing expenses, general expenses, and, yes, rent. But the schedule is still due on Wednesday. And the orders need to be in by 8 AM Sunday morning. And the walk-in broke down last night. And a new spot just opened down the street. The long sail of a restaurant will test your ability to grow, flex, change, adjust, and stay consistent. Your ability to do these things determines if you are to sink like a stone or float along with the breeze.

• 13 •

Worth Yer Salt

Found Oyster received its first review on January 30, 2020. And it was on that date that we first saw our beloved little restaurant in the *LA Times*. The four of us convened along the Found Oyster bar to read the review. In *print*, no less. Still a more tangible and exhilarating experience than anything digital could ever be. Giggling nervously as we prepared ourselves, we knew the impact of the review would be significant. For better. Or for worse . . .

"OK, guys. Here we go . . ." Holly ruffled open the paper.

"Holy shit," Joe murmured.

Holly read the title aloud: "*Tiny East Hollywood haven Found Oyster feels like a refuge and a party.*"

The four of us sat in silence. Then Holly regained her breath. "Holy shit. *Holy shit!* Guys! He got it! He got *us*!"

"*A refuge and a party*," I exclaimed, melting with relief.

"That is a really fucking good title." I could tell Ari's relief equaled my own. "He really did get it."

"A refuge and a party!" Joe exclaimed while jumping to his feet. "A refuge and a fucking party!"

"*A refuge and a party!*" the four of us shouted in unison. And we embraced. And then we read the rest of the review. And embraced again. And we howled. And then Joe and Ari started to prep extra food for service. Holly opened her laptop to order more plates and glassware. And I sat on a stool and rested my elbows on the bar, and reread Found Oyster's first big break.

And I was very happy. Happy, and enthusiastic. Enthusiastic, and . . . And . . . And . . .

And . . . *Maybe you noticed the date of the review . . .*

Just a few weeks after our positive review, I'd receive an odd phone call from my wife, Leah. She'd told me that the NBA season had been canceled. I told her that she was out of her mind. But soon, I would learn the harsh truth. There would be no avoiding the oncoming storm. And within the first days of the Covid pandemic, Last Word lost its *entire* consulting practice. Soon, we'd be forced to shutter Found Oyster. *Indefinitely.* Our restaurant, an intimate space where people worked and dined in such intentional proximity, was horribly positioned for the physical spacing required during the pandemic. What had taken nearly a decade to build turned to ash in what felt like seconds. There were no guests to serve. No clients to sign. No restaurants to open. *Nothing.* We were floating along the surface. Face down. Looking into the unceasing depths of a brooding, unfriendly sea.

And from satiating success to definite doom, the four of us were suddenly split from each other, our team, and the restaurant. In those early days, it was tempting, easy even, to admit defeat. To accept Covid as a sign from the heavens and simply walk away. It was tempting to go find somebody else to rely on. To take a different path. An easier path. Shit, *any path but this path.* And for the first time, it felt like we'd lost any semblance of control. That's just the way things were.

But we didn't quit. And once emergency loans were issued, we wrapped our heads in masks and mobile sneeze guards and got back into the mix. And we decided to flip the brand. *Again.* In the same space that housed the Clam Shack and then Found Oyster was now Overboard—our *third* concept in the same room. We sold buckets of Ari's fried chicken and easily transportable sides. We hosted a weekly seafood market. With the permitting process expedited to allow for Covid-friendly adjustments, our entire dining room transformed into a chicken-frying assembly line. We installed a takeaway window next to the front door. We created a new logo featuring a drunken sailor, clinging, unsuccessfully, to his life preserver. And we found ourselves back where we started. Surviving. But we were in it together. And together we are, still.

Time and Seasoning

Restaurant life is funny. Sometimes it drags likes a barge. Other times, it rips like a Jet Ski. In the years that have passed since opening Found Oyster, I've ridden both vessels. And when I look back I see an earlier version of myself, the one that opened Found Oyster, looking so similar, and yet so different, from the face I see in the mirror today.

That earlier version of me thought he'd seen everything. That version felt so experienced. That version of me *knew* how well versed he was in the world of restaurants. Prepared for anything, he believed. But in truth, that version of me had yet to be tested. That version of me hadn't watched one of his dreams come true only to see it die. And then watch that dream rise yet again. That version of me hadn't fully accepted that a career in restaurants is persistently turbulent. And even when waters appear calm, there is *always* chop ahead. A storm, somewhere on the horizon. But as rough as things can *and will* be, learning to ride the waves is the only way to survive the long voyage of restaurants. And these days, I'm content to let the currents take me where they will. I'm at peace with the lack of certainty. These days, *I float.* And when I look in the mirror these days, the version I see is the same old me, but different. Different, and dare I say, better.

Found Oyster is different now, too. And I do dare say better. We've gained a patio—"the Boat Deck" we call it—in what used to be two metered parking spots. This was an absolutely life-changing development set in motion by the Covid era and proof that municipalities have the power to make business better on Main St. Much of our original staff has moved on. But some remain. And others have joined and become as much a part of Found Oyster's story as anyone who came before. Dishes have come and gone, too. Sometimes successfully (see, beef tartar burger), others less so (see, our desire to feature Massachusetts steamer clams smashed by the smashing of their brittle shells in transit). And where Found Oyster once stood as a bastion for the first-come, first-serve, no-reservations people of the world, our reputation began to grow as a long-line, can't-get-a-seat kind of place that's not actually as busy as it used to be. So, we started taking reservations. And we hold seats for walk-ins. It only took five years for us to start offering both.

Now, there is much else I could tell you about Found Oyster and the things that have changed since we first opened and then survived that cursed pandemic. I have stories of all kinds. We've had great days. And terrible ones. Busy days. And days when most of our seats sat assless. We've survived natural disasters. And national awards. Civil unrest. And competing oyster bars. We battle, every day, to this very day, the constant challenge of growing older. And Found Oyster, for such a little room, has seen a little bit of everything over the years. But everything that's taken place since those early days, every story and obstacle and celebration, is but a single example of restaurant life. Every story is different. *Yours will be, too.* To open a restaurant successfully, you'll need to be prepared to flow with the tide. To take each day in stride and keep striving towards your dreams.

Last Word is different now, too. And yes, *better.* After the success of Found Oyster, we grew. Never repeating brands, but rather investing in the idea of neighborhood restaurants worth traveling for. Each new restaurant, defined by its own sense of community. And strengthened, always, by partnerships. Combining into an ever-expanding portfolio of unique, *real* places, represented by *real* people. Sometimes with new chefs and managers. Mostly with people we've worked with before. And I would not hesitate to say that our crew is the most badass, take-no-prisoners, committed group of folks there ever was. Businesspeople, but artists. Tradesfolk, but local celebrities. Caregivers, but creators. My favorite kind of people. *Restaurant people.* Accept no substitutes. For to be successful in this business, you need to have *great* people around you. I'd be lying if I said that anything less would do.

And that's what I've tried to do. To surround myself with great people. And I *do* dare say that I've done so. As a crew, we'll open more restaurants. We're good at that. How they'll stand the test of time? Well, you've already heard my thoughts on prognosticating success in the restaurant business. The restaurant business is tough. And it will always be tough.

Restaurants Are Hard. Hard Is *Good*.

In restaurants, as in life, you, too, need to be tough. Not in a machismo, "I can take anybody!" kind of way. But with an attitude of "I've had my ass kicked plenty, and I'm still here." Opening a place of your own is bound to be a comedy of errors. It's unavoidable, really. Each new day will present a new set of challenges and, sometimes, you'll falter. Service will suffer. Guests will complain. The power will go out. The chef will walk out. Your bestselling dish will sell out five minutes into service. And with so many new hazards to navigate, it's inevitable that you will fuck up and fall down and make mistakes and screw the pooch.

So? So what? You're human. And so is everybody else working in a restaurant. And so is everybody else dining in a restaurant. And with so much humanity in a place so small, there are bound to be times when everything goes to shit. And it's in these moments, these most challenging of moments when it feels like the world is crashing down around you, that you must remember *why* you're doing this work. These are the moments that will test your resolve. And test your love for this work. And in these moments, you need to remember that this work is hard. *You're doing something hard.* And doing something hard is beautiful. By being the most passionate, empathetic, creative, hospitable, long-thinking, tough-as-nails SOB that ever cooked a dish or carried a tray or washed a pot or shook a cocktail or opened a place of their own, you will survive. You will succeed. And even it doesn't happen at first—*and it almost never does*—you will stay the course until you get the life, or restaurant, that you want. If you're tough enough and committed enough and willing to learn from your stumbles, you will succeed—in anything that you want.

EPILOGUE
Stuff That Matters

I walked off a sleepless red-eye and into Boston's Logan Airport. Peeling my swamped T-shirt from my back, I texted Leah of my safe arrival, trudged my way out of the terminal, and submerged into the back seat of a rideshare. My driver, whose superhuman scale and accent left no doubt of his Eastern European origin, saw our destination load in his phone. His eyes met mine in the rearview mirror.

"Going to the hospital right from the airport?"

"Yeah, man." I paused to compose myself. "Last place in the world I want to be going right now. But I gotta go."

My new guide looked back to his phone, pulled the car into gear, and we headed toward the exit. His eyes concernedly bounced between the road and the rearview mirror. "I'm sorry, Adam." He had learned my name from the app. "It is very serious?"

"Yes. It is. It's serious. Very serious. My oldest friend—" I choked gently on the answer. "My best friend was just diagnosed with some nasty kind of cancer." I felt tears rolling down my cheeks.

"Oh, fuck . . ."

"Oh, fuck, indeed." I rested my head on the window as we emerged from the Sumner Tunnel and onto the winding horse-car path of the clusterfuck that is Storrow Drive. And looking out on the Charles River, usually a source of inspiration and vaguely melancholy nostalgia, I saw only a flowing body of water.

"I am very sorry, Adam. I hope they will beat it, yes? They are young?"

"He is. Thirty-eight, man. Married. With two young boys . . ."

"*Oh, fuck* . . ."

By September 2023, much of life at Found Oyster had returned to normal. Long gone were the days of to-go bags, spacing requirements, and medical uniforms of our Covid-shaped, *Overboard* era. Service had returned to its intended form. And with the pandemic having left Last Word's consulting practice in shambles, Holly and I had decided not to revive that part of the company. Instead, we focused on our expanded growth as a restaurant group. Our most recent opening had been Found Oyster's younger, larger sibling, Queen's Raw Bar. And one of Queen's first investors had been my friend Mike Simari. This was my third visit home to see him in as many months. And the prognosis was terrifying.

Mike had been diagnosed with NUT carcinoma. A rare form of cancer, the severity of which I learned from the staggering concern on the faces of those who knew more. My friend

Mike, an Irish Italian kid who was built like a brick, had a bovine habit of grazing raw vegetables, and could make you laugh at a funeral, would not be spared. And for those of us who loved him, we were forced to watch this rock of a human erode with unnatural haste. But Mike, in the final months of his life, and despite the constant drudging companion of a cart delivering intravenous drugs that kept him alive, *served* his hospital room. Even though we showed up for him, it was Mike who often cared for us.

And it was these little moments—Mike, carving up a Harrison's Roast Beef "three way" to share with nurses; or cracking a beer and miming a sommelier's deep contemplation before passing it off; or storing candy and coffee and Dr. McGillicuddy's Mentholmint Schnapps gifted from friends to calm other, more nervous friends; or telling one of his dirty jokes, so inappropriate and perfectly timed that it broke even the most awful moments of medical sterility into that most visceral of human behavior. *Laughter.* And these memories of being served by my best friend, who was choosing to take care of *others* during his final moments, would become etched in my mind forever. This was simple stuff. *But it's the simple stuff that matters in the end.* When no questions remain about what is important and what is not. It's these seemingly insignificant but immensely important little moments that matter. The tiniest kindnesses that reveal so much more than the act itself. *To care for and be cared for*. That's what it's all about.

And that care extended further than what was occurring in Boston. All the time I was back east, my partners, and my family, had my back. When I was needed in Boston, I was in Boston. Flying out in the middle of the night with nothing more than wishes of support and assurances that things back in LA would be taken care of. And the time I was able to spend with Mike in those final days was in large part because of the support of my wife, my son, Holly, Joe, Ari, and the partners at our other restaurants. Nobody asked if I'd gotten my work done. Nobody asked if I was going to fall behind. Nobody asked if we would lose money in my absence. *Go take care of your friend.* That's all I heard.

And often straight from the hospital, I returned to yet another Edward Hopper storefront of antiqued wood and glass. Entering beneath a simple, martini-glass sign, perched upon a well-worn, wooden barstool, I found my only respite. Comforted, however mildly, by Negronis on hunks of ice and steak frites with funky blue cheese in a jet-black Bordelaise. The Franklin Café, in Boston's South End, acted as my only escape from reality. Over and over, I returned. And on each visit, I would enter into the waterspout chaos of a packed bar. With waves of people swirling into an inescapable wash. And I would miraculously find a single stool. Often cramped in the corner or perilously positioned near the wait station. But a seat. Just for me. Just when I needed it. A much-needed moment of light in a world that was feeling very, very dark.

And it was in these moments, sitting sad and alone and suddenly not alone and less sad, that I was overwhelmed with *gratitude*. A new appreciation of life that I'd learned from Mike. You see, in Mike's final months, he didn't miss watching TV.

He didn't miss scrolling through social media. He had no fear of missing out on world affairs. He wanted to be with his wife and his boys. And his family. And his friends. And he wanted to feel the warm rays of the sun on his face. Or the crisp coldness of a beer in a bar. Or to cook dinners for loved ones that he'd learned, almost by osmosis, from his Italian immigrant father, Frank. Mike was going to miss *people*. Mostly, the ones he loved. And as I sat upon my ancient barstool, watching life go by, I recognized the act of serving, and being served, something to eat and something to drink, is not an optional part of a joyful life. It is *vital*. It's something we all miss when it is our time to go. A comfortable place. People to care for. And to be cared for by people. Nourishment. Love. Respect. Good, simple, and *real*.

When I returned to LA after that third and most terrible of visits, I began to wonder what would have happened to me without the Franklin Café. Not a religious guy, my family far away, I wondered what it would have been like, I *still* wonder what it would have been like, without the reprieve I found during those hard days and nights. Where else would I have gone? What else may have soothed me? I still don't know.

What I *do know* is that there is no replacement for restaurants. It's the humanity that defines them. It's the people that make the place. My favorite neighborhood joints have the right neighborhood joint staff *and* the right neighborhood joint crowd. My favorite diners, the appropriate human fixtures. As attached to the restaurant as their associated counters, wait stations, booths, and stools. My favorite pubs, maintaining a crew, *and regulars*, whose patronage goes back and back and back until they become as attached as the front door. It is the *human* aspect of restaurants that make them so compelling. A human story, rewritten every day. To be drafted by those who dream to own, work, or dine, in one of the world's greatest inventions: *restaurants*. As necessary to the human spirit, experience, and community as any of the great pillars of civilization. Never at the forefront. But always present. An ancient custom, initiated, expanded, and maintained by nearly every culture in the world.

And with great loss, I craved birth. I wanted to make something new. Something that would push me to the limits of my abilities. Something meaningful. The result was this book. And with no previous experience writing books, I began this voyage like so many voyages I've committed to in my life. With absolutely no clarity on where it was heading.

At first, I starting writing a traditional business book. It would provide a soup-to-nuts rundown of a restaurant opening. But then I realized that without the *people* around me, I have no idea how things would've turned out. The theories I'd written felt hollow without the human beings that made those theories work. So, I kept writing. And at some point, I discovered the simple truth. My life has been filled with ups and downs. But it's *how* I've taken my lumps, and *whom* I've taken them with, that has most shaped me as a person.

Now, I can't tell you what it feels like to win and never look back. For that is an experience I've never felt. But I can tell you this: I do things I love. Make things I love. Go places I love. With people I love. And I let nothing stand in the way of that. And although my path has never been easy, and I've yet to ride a single straightaway, it's the only path I'd ever walk. My own path. And directly next to those I care about. And that's enough for me.

And that's enough about me. What you do with this book is up to you. But if I were to have my wish, you'd use it to make *something*. Maybe a restaurant. Maybe not. But as long as it's something *you* make, and *you* love, well, that would make *me* very happy.

I wish you the best. Make stuff. Be happy. And never give up.

ACKNOWLEDGMENTS

For giving me, and much of the world, something to do. For being there for me, and for everybody, all the damn time. For working so that others can party. Restaurant people. Thanks.

For letting me be me. For creating a life that I wake up to, fully content, every day. For picking me up when I'm down and being strong when I'm weak and for being the loves of my life. Leah and Owen. Thanks.

For sticking with me through good times and bad. For being as good of a friend as a partner. For being the most creative restaurant maker I ever met. For being fully and totally you. Holly Fox. Thanks.

For making this book look the way this book looks. For working on cover art from a wedding on a tablet. For being a real friend and a fantastic illustrator. Davin Sanchez. Thanks.

For being the most badass, no-bullshit, real-deal restaurant people that there ever were, are, or will be. For making me look good. For caring. Joe, Ari, Santos, and the rest of the LWH partners and team. Thanks.

For believing in me as a writer before I believed in myself. For being honest and constructive and endlessly supportive. For being there from start to finish. David Parker and the rest of the Parker fam. Thanks.

For centering my ideas into a central narrative. For gentle nudges that the writing could improve. For literary inspiration, conversation, good wine, and firsthand Celtics knowledge. Baxter Holmes. Thanks.

For putting up serious money with serious risk. For being there and stepping up when nothing was guaranteed. For being the first ones to see something special in us. To all the Found Oyster and Last Word investors. Thanks.

For supporting Holly, me, and Last Word like nobody else. For your unwavering support, trust, and providing us with the opportunity to do things differently. For being a great mentor as well as partner. Mike Glick. Thanks.

For making this whole thing happen. For taking a call from an unpublished restaurant guy and believing and believing and believing and hustling until it did happen. For listening to me ramble, whenever I needed to ramble. Leila Campoli. Thanks.

For taking a chance on a restaurant story. For putting in the long hours to make this book better. For honesty, clear feedback, and understanding. For making me a better writer. Matt Holt, Katie Dickman, and the rest of the BenBella / Matt Holt team. Thanks.

For sticking with me when I was at my worst. For bailing me out and keeping me grounded and not giving up. For love going back further than I can remember. My mom and dad and sister. Thanks.

For being my second family and never putting me second. For love, fun, camaraderie, and laughter. For a place that feels like home and tastes like home and, now, is home. Anne, Bevan, Nick, Sian, and the rest of my Bunch family. Thanks.

For being there, no matter what. Like seriously, no matter what. For being too funny to be real and too real to be made up. For loyalty and shit talking like no other. LaBroad, JB, Digi, Sean, Mikey Z, Cait, and the rest of my Masshole hooligans. Thanks.

For being the inspiration for this book. For everything I remember and for everything I don't. For burning bright, maybe too bright, and for forever changing my world. Mike Simari and Jeffery Murphy. I miss you. Thanks.

For the buy-in. For the wild Saturday nights. The anniversaries. The birthdays. The friends gathering along the bar. The lovers playing footsie. For everyone who parts with their hard-earned cash in support of restaurants and small businesses of all kinds. Thanks.

For reading. For keeping the old art form alive through the ancient activity of reading books. For writers. For taking the time to make something pretty out of words. For readers and writers and everyone who enriches our world with honesty, wit, and stories. Thanks.

ABOUT THE AUTHOR

Photography by Jen Rosenstein

A longtime Los Angeles resident, Adam Weisblatt is a proud son of the great state of Massachusetts, husband to Leah June and father to Owen Arlo, professional diner, and lover of lobster rolls, sherry, guitars, and antiques of all kinds. Since cofounding Last Word Hospitality with Holly Fox as a consulting company in 2014, Weisblatt and his partners have now launched some of Southern California's most beloved restaurants including Found Oyster, Barra Santos, Queen's Raw Bar and Grill, Hermon's, Rasarumah, the Red Dog Pioneertown, and The Copper Room. Weisblatt is a board member of the Independent Hospitality Coalition.